THE
CELEBRITY
CEO

THE
CELEBRITY
CEO

**How Entrepreneurs Can Thrive by Building
a Community and a Strong Personal Brand**

RAMON RAY

Indigo River Publishing

Editors: Tanner Chau and Regina Cornell
Cover Design: Dissect Designs
Interior Design: mycustombookcover.com

Indigo River Publishing
3 West Garden Street, Ste. 352
Pensacola, FL 32502
www.indigoriverpublishing.com

Ordering Information:
Quantity sales: Special discounts are available on quantity purchases by corporations, associations, and others. For details, contact the publisher at the address above.

Orders by US trade bookstores and wholesalers: Please contact the publisher at the address above.

Printed in the United States of America

Library of Congress Control Number: 2019936224

ISBN: 978-1-948080-85-9

First Edition

With Indigo River Publishing, you can always expect great books, strong voices, and meaningful messages. Most importantly, you'll always find . . . words worth reading.

Special thanks to my dear family for their patience with me and their love—Ronnie, my wife of over 25 years; Tim and Charity, my dear children; Mom (Olivia); and Joanna and Clalin, my sisters.

Most of all, thank you, Jesus Christ, for your strength and guidance in my life.

TABLE OF CONTENTS

FACEBOOK

TIPS FOR EVERY SOCIAL PLATFORM

RACHEL MICHAELOV, THE TAX EXPERT

ADRIAN MILLER, THE SALES TRAINER AND BUSINESS STRATEGIST

PERSONAL BRANDING'S SMALL GIANTS

Part III: From Small Screen To Stage

HOW CAN YOU SPEAK AT EVENTS

PART I

THE MIND-SET OF A CELEBRITY

1

The Making of a Celebrity CEO

In the spring of 2014, I received an email inviting me to speak at an event in Aruba. I assumed it was spam and ignored it. A few days later, I received an update to that email, asking me again to come to Aruba and speak. I ignored that email as well. After a few more days, I received a *third* email with the same invitation. I replied, and the rest is history. I ended up speaking in front of almost a thousand Aruban professionals.

I hadn't requested to speak. I wasn't searching for my next speaking engagement. Someone running this event saw me online, researched me a bit, and invited me to speak. This is the result of having a strong personal brand. You aren't chasing after business. Instead, clients will begin to chase you down to work with you. You can be choosy and pick whom *you* want to work with. You don't have to lower your prices to get the next gig.

I've been asked by fledgling business owners how I got

to be so successful in my business and able to work with some of the biggest brands in the world. There are several reasons. My clients tell me I'm easy to work with. The thousands of attendees at the events I speak at have expressed that they enjoy the way I connect with the audience. The most important reason why I have clients chasing after me is that I have created a fan base that is always growing. From this fan base, I get new and repeat clients. I'm very well known to my audience because of my presence online and in person.

I'm a "celebrity CEO." A celebrity CEO can be defined as a business owner who has a growing community of engaged fans (not customers) who follow the business owner (via email newsletter, social media, or by attending events, etc.) in order to learn from him or her. A percentage of these fans are converted into regular paying customers. I'm a business owner, a business professional, and I have a community of fans. This community lives largely on Facebook and Twitter, but also via my email list and websites. **This community is not for my vanity, but it's a source of customers and referrals that I leverage on a constant basis to grow my business.** In this book, I'm going to share with you some of the key best practices, tips, and insight for how YOU can achieve these results and become a celebrity CEO. Over the years, I've built a very strong and recognizable personal brand for "Ramon Ray," and this has attracted a following and a fan base. Within this fan base are paying customers.

Origin Story

I can remember how I felt when I had no other option left to become the person I am today. For several years, I had been working at the United Nations, and at the same time, I was running my own business. The UN does not allow its staff to have private enterprises without special permission. For years I had this permission, but then things changed. I was asked to shut down my business. I didn't know it then, but I was first and foremost an entrepreneur, with the craving of starting and nurturing my own businesses, putting teams together, taking risks, and creating mini-ventures.

I didn't close my business; therefore, my contract with the United Nations ended. It was equivalent to being fired for being an entrepreneur. After more than ten years of service, I no longer had a day job. What was I to do? Thankfully, over the years I had a few clients who sponsored events I had organized and hired me to do webinars. But I had to do more. No longer did I have a steady job with a steady paycheck. I went from having a part-time side hustle to becoming a full-time entrepreneur, all while trying to provide for my young family. This had to work; there was no Plan B. Even if there was another option, the hunger for running my own full-time business was too intense to ignore.

At the time, I didn't know the term *personal branding*—marketing myself and my career as a brand. I didn't know about marketing automation, sales-funnel target marketing—or anything. However, I did know what I was good at, and I had the confidence to go for it. I was good at speaking on stage, organizing events, selling, and communicating. Putting these skills together birthed and has grown what I've been successfully doing for many years: hosting events sponsored by leading brands and being paid to speak to thousands of business owners and professionals every year.

I'm going to tell you why building a fan base is important later in the book. I want to first share with you my early successes of personal branding with **fan building** through a simple email newsletter. I still publish a regular email newsletter, and it's been well over fifteen years since I sent out the first one. It was called Small Business Technology Report. It was based on interviews I would do with executives from technology companies who shared their insight about marketing to small businesses with other executives. Everyone wants to know what everyone else is doing. In hindsight, this was a brilliant start, but I didn't realize it at the time. So what was I doing?

I had a narrow target market (we'll talk about this later in the book), focused on a very specific topic. This meant that the head of small business marketing at Dell, for example, would be really interested in reading my newsletter if it featured the head of small business marketing at Microsoft. Over the years I built a following, a fan base, a community of executives who wanted to read my content.

And this is where it all began—with a simple email newsletter. Today, of course, there are multiple social media platforms and a variety of options you can use to spread your message to a community. People ask me how I've been so successful in working with leading brands. I believe the number one marketing secret for my success is my steady focus on a very particular, or niche, market.

I remember my interview with President Obama in his first live video chat. Out of three hundred thousand applicants to interview the president, I was one of five who were chosen. Want to guess what my question was? Yup, that's right—something related to small business. If you search on YouTube for "Your Interview with the President Recap - 2012," you can see the interview.

Finding a niche and targeting a highly specific market is a powerful concept that you can, and should, consider for your business. This doesn't mean you can't expand or grow, but for us *very* small business owners, we have limited resources. Limited time and money. Instead of pouring all your energy into trying to be everything to everybody, pour your energy into being the very best for a specific group of people.

While in a rush to get more income, sometimes we're tempted to say yes to everyone. We're tempted to be an accountant who does accounting for auto mechanics, bookkeeping for lawyers, and audits for elementary schools. I know the fear of needing to make this month's rent or pay your staff or buy gifts for the holidays. But, *trust me*, for the long term, it's much better to be the accountant focused on audits for elementary schools. You become an **expert** in all things elementary school accounting, and all the elementary school principals will start referring you.

In the early years of growing my personal brand, of being the Celebrity CEO, I also learned the importance of media attention. Again, I didn't know the fancy terms I know now, and I didn't know how important it was. I was just excited to be on TV or be on the radio or be referenced in a magazine or newspaper.

Want to take a walk with me back in time? Over seventeen years ago, Entrepreneur.com featured me in an article about information technology consultants:

> *The Internet can be an invaluable resource for finding a competent, reliable ITC* [information technology consultant] *in your area, but like most products and services advertised in cyberspace, you shouldn't take what you see*

at face value, according to Ramon Ray, small-business technology analyst and consultant, founder and CEO of Family Computer Consulting Services in New York City and publisher of the online newsletter Smallbiztechnology. com. "There are a lot of places on the Net where you can find consultants, but just because they have a nice-looking Web site, that doesn't tell you if the guy is a scam artist or if he just got out of jail," says Ray. "That's where word of mouth comes into play. If [an ITC] can provide you with the name of a client you've heard of, or if your own network of friends can say good things about this guy, I would rely on that. You should also ask for references. If [the ITC] is good, they'll be prepared to give you some. And if they don't have references, that can also be a good indicator."[1]

It was articles like this that helped solidify and build my credibility as a small business expert (or whatever you want to call it) in the community of small business owners, entrepreneurs, and the brands who wanted to reach them. The concepts we're going to talk about in this book are much easier to implement than they were in the 1990s (or before) with the saturated ease of access to the Internet, but the principles are the same.

The success I've had in building an extremely strong personal brand has been a long road. It's been a journey. It doesn't happen all at once. Like looking at a recipe book, where all the ingredients and the process is laid out for you, consider *Celebrity CEO* your recipe book for personal branding.

While much of this book focuses on the digital tools

---

[1] https://www.entrepreneur.com/article/23574

you can use to build your personal brand, understand that the personal relationships, emotional intelligence, and ability to connect to another human are even more important.

I can remember the first time I met Joe Connolly of WCBS Radio 88. He was speaking with Jay Walker, the founder of Priceline.com, at an event hosted by the radio station. This was ten or more years ago. I was one of the last people at the event and walked with Joe out of the venue. It was a warm handshake and smile that made the connection—no tweets or Instagram live-stream videos.

In 2002 I interviewed then Senator Hillary Clinton at an event in New York City. While a gaggle of attendees was around her, I went the opposite direction and found her assistant. After some pleasantries, I snagged an interview with her. I asked her questions related to—no surprises here—small businesses. (If you go on YouTube and search "Hillary Clinton - Ramon Ray Interview," you'll find it.) This goes to show you the power of human connections in the real world two years before Facebook, and they are still powerful to this day.

If you're serious about building a community, you have to have the mind-set of a community manager. Before I go on stage and speak at an event, you won't find me in the green room by myself. I'm walking around speaking to attendees to find out about their businesses and their needs. Speaking from a stage and then leaving is easy. But it's essential to show appreciation, respect, and engagement with my fan base. Why are Penn and Teller so loved by fans of their comedy? They stay after their shows and shake hands and chat with the audience.

My journey has been about building a community where

I'm very focused on the expertise I share and deliver. It's been about building a fan base within a particular community. It's been about networking and building relationships. The final part of this journey is, of course, the tools.

My first serious website was SmallBizTechnology. com—I bought the domain in 1999, twenty years ago. I went through a variety of methods to update the website on a regular basis because back then there were no sites like WordPress. On my computer I would launch a software program called FrontPage made by Microsoft. This was before cloud computing. It was the leading do-it-yourself software for building and managing a website. A few times a day, I'd type up a blog post, save it to my computer, and using FTP (file transfer protocol, a method for transferring files via the Internet), I'd update the website.

This was content for my community. I did it without LinkedIn, without one tweet, and with no video (well, except the one with Hillary!). Bottom line: I used an email newsletter and a simple website to share content with my community and grow it. Today, there are a lot more tools, and just about everyone is online.

You, the Celebrity

In some ways, you have it much easier today, but on the other hand, it can be much more difficult. When I was starting out, people were still getting CompuServe diskettes in the mail. There was little online content about much of anything. Today, *everyone* is creating content. Everyone's phones are documenting their dinners, babies' first steps, staff meetings, sales, and more. The hard part is figuring out what you can do to capture the attention of your ideal customers and nurture them to a sale.

You're constantly competing with the president's tweets, your neighbor's viral dog videos, and your teen's video chats. While most of us will never be a celebrity like Oprah Winfrey, Taylor Swift, or Mark Zuckerberg, we all can be celebrities to a specific community. **All business owners can be celebrity CEOs.** I'm blessed to have a strong roster of clients from leading brands that I work with. I'm honored to get calls and emails just about every week asking for an interview on a podcast, blog, or website. It happens because of the power of being a celebrity CEO.

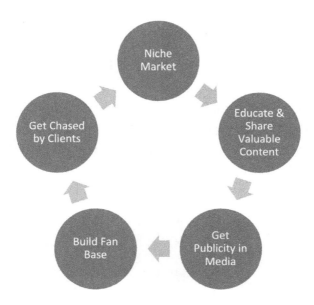

In the simple diagram above you'll see the celebrity CEO road map. Decide on your target market—the niche that is best for you.

1. Create great content that educates and adds value to this market. Do a blog post. Host an event.

2. Get or create publicity (in a family-friendly way). Get an interview on a local radio station. Talk to a reporter. Be interviewed on a local podcast.

3. Your fan base will grow and grow. People start signing up for your email newsletter or following you on social media.

4. Turn fans to clients. Now watch as a percentage of these fans, on a regular basis, turn to customers.

This is what being a celebrity CEO is all about.

Gary Vaynerchuk is probably one of the most famous celebrity CEOs around. He has about five million followers on Instagram and two million on Twitter. Ha! I *only* have about thirty thousand on Twitter. Guess what? It doesn't bother me.

Gary Vaynerchuk, Ramon Ray, and Tim Ray, June 2013

Being a celebrity CEO is about living the life you want that's great for you and your family. If you, like Gary, want to buy the Jets build a global marketing agency, that takes an entirely different strategy, mind-set, and sacrifice than if you're going to work from a home office with a team of five people, which is how I live.

This book won't teach you how to have viral videos or be an Instagram influencer, but it will guide you in how to be better known than your competition and get customers, the right customers, to chase you down. Seth Godin is another celebrity CEO. He's a mega influencer with one of the largest email lists in the world.

Seth Godin and my daughter, 2010

Seth Godin hammers home the importance of building a tribe of people who rally around what you're saying or doing. "People like us do things like this" is one of his core rallying cries. If you follow this principle, you'll start to get the attention of the people whose attention you want. They'll start to sit up and take notice and become your fans, or your tribe or community. Within that community, there will be those who want to know more about the solutions *you* can provide. Why? Because they know, like, and trust you from your online presence. Next step: they'll become customers. Rinse and repeat (refer back to the diagram above).

The more **value** you add to someone's life (value could be content and education), the more **trust** you'll have with him. The more **trust** you establish with someone in the right target market, the higher chance you have of him becoming your **customer**. He will invest his money in **you** to solve his problem and/or provide something to him that he needs.

People often ask me why I create so much video. Well, because it works. The more video I have (which is value/education), the more **trust** I create with my fan base. Video (as we'll talk about more in the book) humanizes and personalizes your brand. I can't shake everyone's hands or be in front of everyone in real life, but video is the next-best thing.

Anyone can do what I've done. If you follow the principles I've outlined in these pages and work hard to make it happen, it will happen. The goal is to be seen as an expert in your field, creating desire from everybody in your professional community to want to work with you. This is a great place to be. Most business professionals fight and claw and scratch to get noticed and be picked. If you have a strong personal brand, you're not the lowly draft hoping to get picked, you're LeBron—everybody wants you.

We live in a very noisy world. Those who can break through that noise by having a strong personal brand will succeed. The marketplace for our products, services, and ideas is constantly filled with a flurry of competing messages, all vying for our attention and the attention of our customers and potential customers. You're trying to get your message about the solutions you offer in front of the right customers, but they're distracted.

And frankly, everyone's distracted. We *only* care about ourselves, about our needs, about what's most important to *us* at a particular moment in time. For instance, we know we must pay our taxes on April 15, but why are accountants only so busy in late March and early April? We only care about taxes when we've got that deadline in our faces. A new couple doesn't buy a crib for their baby when they get married, but Dad and Mom think of buying the crib when there's a bun in the oven. So we're not only distracted overall, but our attention is very cyclical and shifts from hour to hour, day to day, week to week.

The good news for *you*, as a business professional trying to sell your products or services, is that we all have needs. We all have problems, and we all want solutions to those problems. Those needs could be as basic as entertainment—Netflix, Hulu, Amazon, etc., have some solutions for you. Other problems could be the need for a quick meal—Chick-fil-A, McDonald's, Wendy's, and a zillion other restaurants have solved that problem.

You've heard of these solutions because, over the years, these large brands have captured your attention by spending lots of money on advertising and marketing and word of mouth. These brands I've mentioned are, of course, global brands whose names are in the lexicon of just about everyone in the modern world.

Now, what about *your* business?

Maybe you're a local accounting firm in midtown New York City, or you're a distributor of water filtration systems in a suburb of Dallas, Texas. Maybe you serve customers in Portland, Oregon; Hyderabad, India; Sao Paolo, Brazil; or anywhere else in the world. You don't have a large budget to spend on advertising or marketing. You don't have a budget to bombard a local or national market with TV, radio, or online advertising.

That's okay.

Every entrepreneur, every business owner, can be a local celebrity. They can be thought of first by their clients and potential clients. Every professional can build a strong personal brand, which is a great way to ensure that the right customers in need of your solutions know about you and become your customers. Personal branding is not about being a global megastar with zillions of followers, like the Kardashians or some other celebrity. In some cases, successful personal branding is very local. You might not be the most famous real estate agent in the entire United States, but you might be extremely well known in a small suburb of Albany, New York. Or if you're in an incredibly dense city like New York City, maybe you're not known all over the city, but you are quite well known in Park Slope, which is a small section of Brooklyn, New York.

In another case, you might be nationally or globally known, but only to a very thin slice of a particular industry. For example, maybe you're a lawyer in Atlanta, best known for helping high-growth startups incorporate their businesses. That's someone with a strong local personal brand. Or you might be a lawyer specializing in high-rise-apartment-tenant litigation for senior citizens. You might be nationally known but to a very narrow segment of the population.

Make sense?

Maybe you're an expert in carpet cleaning for hotels. While most of the world has no clue who you are, I bet every head of custodial services at major hotels knows just who you are—you're a local celebrity. I was recently giving some advice to a couple who were starting their health-and-fitness business. When they first started out, everything was very general. They wanted to serve everybody. However, as we spoke, they shared that one of their goals was to help those who have special needs, such as amputees or those with mental health issues. I advised them to focus on building their personal brand for this particular market. It would take too much money and time for them to be known by everybody. However, it's quite doable to be the top fitness experts for amputees in the New York City area. That's a local celebrity.

As small business owners, we don't have the time or money to be globally known to everyone. However, we can make a great living by being well known to a targeted, or niche, group of people. Marketing legend Seth Godin calls this "famous to the family." He wrote about the topic in a blog post:[2]

> *There is famous and there is famous to the family. Cousin Aaron is famous to my family. Or, to be less literal, the family of people like us might understand that Satya the milliner or perhaps Sarma Melngailis or Peter Olotka are famous.*

And famous to the family is precisely the goal of just about all marketing now. You don't need to be Nike or Apple or GE. You need to be famous to the small circle of people you are hoping will admire and trust you. Your shoe store needs to be famous to the 300 shoe shoppers in your town. Your retail consulting practice needs to be famous to 100 people at ten major corporations. Your WordPress consulting practice needs to be famous to 650 veterinarians or chiropractors. Famous the way George Clooney and George Washington are famous, but to fewer people.

By famous, I [mean] admired, trusted, given the benefit of the doubt. By famous, I mean seen as irreplaceable or best in the world.

Here's how to tell if you're famous: If I ask someone in your community to name the person who is known for X, will they name you? If I ask about which store or freelancer is the best place, hands down, to get Y, will they name you? If we played 20 questions, could I guess you?

Being famous to the family is far more efficient than being famous to everyone. It takes focus, though.

Famous to the family (of board game fans) is the key to making my friend Peter's Cosmic Encounter Kickstarter hit its goal. Or Ramon Ray's new magazine getting traction. Famous to the family is what this IndieGogo needs in order to change kids' lives. And failing to be famous to the family is precisely why most Kickstarters fail.

Famous to the family is an important concept. Very few of us will be globally famous, like Beyoncé, Jay Z, or even the local chain of cheap hamburger restaurants you may love in your local town. However, we can all be really well known (i.e., famous to the family) in our local community. It's really hard to become globally famous, or even famous in your entire city. However, it's a lot easier to be well known and sought after in your profession or industry. Stop spending so much time trying to be known to everyone. Stop spinning your wheels trying to be a mega TV star. Stop trying to reach every user on Facebook. Instead, **focus.** Focus on the smallest segment you can find, and from there you can expand.

2

Personal Branding 101

As a child, I loved Pop-Tarts. I'm not talking about the grocery store value brand; the *real* Pop-Tarts made by Kellogg's. And like many kids, I also liked Cheerios, the ones made by General Mills. However, I can remember a time in my life when money was tight, and our family bought the "no frills" brand from time to time. Maybe, just maybe, the generic brand tastes the same (I doubt it), but no kid wants a no-frills brand cereal, or any other food. Everyone wants the cereal, or other product, that *looks* delicious, that *looks* inviting, that *looks* amazing. Right? This is what personal branding is all about.

Personal branding is the art and science of being so irresistible and so desirable that your target market wants to buy from you, work for you, be around you, or hear from you. They are *chasing you*. Frankly, they don't want anyone else.

A strong personal brand is more than just about people knowing you're a website developer. That's easy; web developers are a dime a dozen. It's about the right customers knowing you're the best web developer for their needs. This most likely includes not just your technical competence to design websites but your customer service, your design process, and more.

To reiterate, large companies have big budgets to spend lots of money on advertising, sales, and marketing campaigns. They can spend $50,000 or $50 million on advertising to ensure everyone in the USA, or the world, knows who they are. We know their logos and their corporate stories. Even smaller businesses can spend some money to promote their corporate brands. However, a personal brand and corporate brand are two different things.

A corporate brand is about the brand's promise, represented by its logo and imagery. Think Tesla, Polo, McDonald's, Nike. A small business, like you and me —it's all about our personal brand and how the customer feels about us as individuals. For you, a very small business owner, your corporate brand has some importance. Indeed, you want people to know your logo and your brand promise. For most of us, our customers are buying *us*; they're buying our smile, our trust, how we connect and make them feel as individuals. Think of the local graphic design shop, the orthopedic shoe vendor your mother-in-law needs, the copy repair company. For these small companies, for you and me, it's primarily all about us as individuals, about us as people.

It's not about having a flashy business card or a sleek, modern logo. First and foremost it's, how does another human, who has a need in his business or personal life, feel about you, and is he even aware that you have a solution for his need?

This is the essence of personal branding. This is what it means to be a celebrity CEO. McDonald's has its golden arches. We have our handshake and warm smile. Dell has its TV and radio advertising campaign. You have your constant desire to educate customers and showcase how amazing you are for them. Starting and building a strong personal brand is not easy. It takes time and commitment to excellence and the art of self-marketing, promoting yourself like crazy.

In order to do this, you don't need to spend a lot of money—in fact you don't need to spend *any* money. Most businesses are plain vanilla. Nothing is wrong with vanilla ice cream, but for a business to be plain, to be boring, to be unremarkable, is *deadly*. It hurts the business. They're not remarkable; they're not special; it's hard to tell what's different about them. It's hard to tell why *you* should connect with one business and not another.

Do this small test: Who are your top three competitors? Write it down.

What can you do, or what are you doing, to be just a little bit better than your competition, and hopefully a *lot* better? Entrepreneur and author Peter Shankman often asks attendees this in his speeches: When you go on a flight, you're happy if the plane lands safely and you get some peanuts. Right? That's all you expect. But companies like Virgin do their best to make it an *experience*. They're doing things just a bit better or a bit differently than the competition. While being a celebrity CEO takes a lot of work, effort, persistence, and thoughtfulness, part of it is pretty simple. While everyone else is just okay, you need to be a bit better than okay to make a difference in your customers' minds.

Let's unpack this a bit more: I've been told by brand

executives and others that they love my style of interviewing. It makes them feel comfortable during the interview, and they're able to freely talk with me in a natural conversation. There are *a lot* of people who do interviews; however, my interview style is different than others'. It's fun, high energy, and very conversational and relatable.

Think of your business and your brand. What's that one thing, or many things, you can do just a bit differently than everyone else?

Here's another tip from "Ramon's playbook" of being a celebrity CEO: I like to wear bright colors. It's not a gimmick, it's me, but it works. There is a picture of me wearing my signature bright-blue sweater on my Twitter.

You want to be different and stand out in two main areas. First, before people even speak with you or hear about you, what does your visual and nonverbal brand tell people? If you have a business card, what does it say? How does your website represent your expertise? Second, when people do connect and interact with you, what are you conveying to them? How do you make them feel?

Since much of your competition is either so unremarkable or provides a terrible customer experience, or both, you have to be more proactive and mindful to build a better personal brand and to get the attention of customers who need what you sell!

Going back to my earlier example about Pop-Tarts—the product inside the box was essentially the same as the off brand's; however, one brand added color, design, and excitement to their product and the other didn't. Your personal brand must stand out, pop, and sizzle, at least in a way that sets you apart from your competitors and that is in alignment with the integrity of your brand's values. Let's try an example.

Maybe you're the owner of a local upholstery cleaning company and you're looking to be a celebrity CEO. You ensure that all of your employees say please and thank you, and cover their shoes with booties before walking onto a client's carpet. Maybe after each job you visit the client, say thank you, bring a fresh bouquet of flowers, and take a selfie with the customer. Over time, your celebrity CEO status, your overall brand, is going to *increase* because you're doing something another company doesn't do (like leaving fresh flowers). On top of that, it's part of your mission to go above and beyond for your customers!

A strong personal brand conveys two things to your customers and potential customers: (1) you have the solution they're looking for, and (2) out of all the places customers could buy from, you stand out as the best option for their needs. A strong personal brand makes YOU pop, sizzle, bling, and sparkle. A strong personal brand helps customers *see* you in a crowded and noisy marketplace and choose YOU (and your business) as the solution to their needs.

A large part of the success of starting and building your personal brand today is about your digital marketing. It's how you educate your customers over time and consistently. This is the power of **personal branding**. Let me share another illustration of the power of a strong personal brand: I travel around the world, and I am often in unfamiliar locations—be it in the USA, India, or another place. When in doubt about what products or services I should purchase for my personal needs, I tend to look first for familiar brands. For example, if I'm landing in another country, with no hotel recommendations and not sure where to stay, I prefer to stay in a Hilton, Marriot, or another American brand because it's what I'm most familiar with. Does this mean a local hotel chain is no good? Not at all. It just means that when I'm not sure what to do, I'll default to what I do know. This is the mind-set of almost every consumer out there.

If you have a strong personal brand, those prospective customers who are not sure who to choose will choose you over your competition. This is how your personal brand works with your customers and potential customers. The market for your products or services is crowded, noisy, and unfamiliar. Your potential customers are often not sure what to buy or who to turn to. By having a strong personal brand, you reduce their uncertainty and fear while increasing their confidence in buying from you.

If someone is looking for accounting services and you are the accountant she's heard the most about and seen the most of, you have a greater chance of being chosen instead of your competitor. In a sea of unknown brands, the brand with the most credibility and trust will win the business. If you don't win someone's business *today*, do not be discouraged. Stay consistent in the value you offer to ensure that you're at the top of her mind and will get her business at some point in the future.

Why do companies spend billions of dollars on advertising? They do this to ensure their brand is at the forefront of the prospect's mind. On the radio, where I live, I hear ads for Bob's Discount Furniture quite often. When I'm looking to buy furniture, don't you think Bob's Discount Furniture is on my mind? All of this advertising is to build brand recognition. With personal branding, instead of advertising on the

TV or radio, it's about doing specific actions to get attention and showcase yourself using events, books, social media, and tools. This is the power of personal branding.

What about your current customers and those who are very familiar with you or know a lot about the products or services they're looking for? A strong personal brand is still essential. For educated customers who already know you, they'll still choose *you*, as your brand appears most credible, most experienced, and the most desirable. For sure, all customers are not for you, but you're not aiming for all customers, right? You want those customers who fit a particular profile.

When you raise your hand, take a stand, and have a specific point of view, you attract people to you who identify with your message. Remember, as Seth Godin often says, "People like us do things like this." As you seek to start and build your personal brand, remember that you can't reach everyone in the world, nor should you want to. You couldn't service everyone, at least not as a very small business.

As you build your personal brand, show how unique you are, and showcase your version of the world (like the Pop-Tarts example), you attract people to you who are a perfect fit. Large brands can amass large groups of people to be their customers—thousands, millions, hundreds of millions. They can also sell to the masses. As smaller businesses, as smaller brands, we, for the most part, want to sell to a much smaller segment of the market. A powerful personal brand helps us to not just sell stuff to the market but also to enable potential customers to self-select to work with us.

Let's take music for example. I love a certain type of gospel music. I don't like all music and certainly not all types of gospel music. Those musicians who create the type of music I like use all the channels they can to ensure they get my attention. Your business is no different.

Maybe you're a local computer repair technician in Orlando, Florida. Let's pretend you have guaranteed-on-time service, your team wears crisp-looking uniforms, and you give each computer a free cleaning. One more thing: you charge premium prices. You are not for *every* business in Orlando that has computer troubles. Some might want really cheap technicians, and maybe they're not as good as you are. But those who want the best service, which you offer, are going to be attracted to you and pay for it.

This is the power of personal branding. It's not just using social media to educate your customers and get their attention, although this is a vital component.

FISH. SMALL POND.

Those with a very strong personal brand are incredibly clear on *who* their ideal customer is. They're incredibly clear on who their target market is. While national brands are targeting broad swaths of customers, we small business owners do best when we go narrow, very narrow, and then expand from there.

We do our best when we're a fish in a very small pond, as opposed to being a fish in a very big pond. The more you can narrow down and get *very* specific on who your customer is, the smaller your pond will get and the bigger fish you will be.

Let's say you own a local hair salon for women. Sure, in some ways you want every woman who needs her hair done to be a patron of your salon; however, here are the benefits of catering to a much narrower clientele than "women who need their hair done": You can specialize your service to women with a certain type of hair. You might think, "Ramon, I'll lose the business of the women who don't fit into my profile." That is correct. However, you will begin to *gain* so many more women who have the type of hair that you *do* cater to. More and more women who have the type of hair you cater to will spread the word to their friends and encourage them to come to your salon.

The narrower the audience you cater to, the more specialized you and your team become. If you need a heart transplant, do you want surgery from a general practitioner, or do you want the expertise of a doctor who focuses only on heart surgery and has done many more such surgeries than the general practitioner?

You can quickly get rid of the *maybes* and get to the *yeses*. When a woman is considering getting her hair done, she has three considerations to make regarding your salon: she *might* come, she *won't* come, or she *will* come to your salon. By being very specific in the *type* of hair you work on, you will help women make fast decisions about your business. This is good. Honda owners don't sit in front of a Mercedes dealership wondering if they can help. They don't even give it consideration. They instead seek out a Honda dealer. Make sense?

As a family, we've moved a few times, and wherever we end up, there are always hair salons. However, my wife always looks for Dominican hair salons because she likes how they do hair. Sure, there are hair salons that just say "hair salon," but the Dominican ones are doing really well. Why? They know there are plenty of women who are looking specifically for Dominican hair salons. They're always packed and have a steady flow of business.

It's immensely helpful to build one or more customer personas of the type of customer, or group of customers, you best serve. Let's say you have a carpet cleaning business. Who is your ideal type of customer? Is it "everyone who has a home"? *No!* Instead it could be something like this:

- Female (My guess is most carpet-cleaning decisions are made by the lady of the house!)

- Household income of $250,000 a year (I'm just making that up; it could be higher or lower.)

- Has owned their home for ten years or more

- Has three or more children

- Has a pet

- Likes to entertain friends

- Has four bedrooms or more

Does this mean that you won't or can't serve those who don't fall into this category? Of course not. But it means that you can begin to create marketing that best speaks to this type of customer. You can create surveys that might help to identify this type of customer. To create a great survey, first understand *what* information you need to segment your customers. The shorter your survey is, the more likely it is to get a response. You can use a tool such as SurveyMonkey, Typeform, Google Forms, or Zoho to ask a question.

Maybe you ask for first name, email, and two or three questions to place your customers into "buckets," or segments. Maybe you ask a demographic question such as gender or age. Maybe you ask a psychographic question, like what kind of music they listen to or if they like sports or not. Now that you have this intelligence you can begin to target people like this and market to them. Make sense? As you get more and more people as customers, you can keep using surveys to ensure you're always serving the right customers.

This doesn't mean that you can't have a few target audiences, but start small and then grow. Don't just rely on demographics to target your customers. Demographics refer to how we look on the outside: black, white, Spanish, Chinese, etc. What's just as important, or more important, as demographics are psychographics.

I bet those people in your town with household incomes of $250K or more and four-bedroom homes might work in similar places and have similar social circles. They'll begin to refer your company to their friends.

So now, instead of being a business that cleans the carpet of "any home" or "any apartment," you're a BIG FISH in a SMALL POND and a specialist in cleaning carpets for certain homes owned by certain people. You might start off by building one type of customer profile. As you get better at this, you might end up with two or three distinct types of customers you can serve.

When I go to a big event like SXSW, held annually in Austin, Texas, a few people know me. I'm a small fish in a very big pond. However, when I attend an even like the B2SMB Conference, an event for large brands who are selling to small businesses, about half the room knows me.

Why? I've invested a lot of time in this niche industry and know all the players. Sure, McDonald's needs to sell billions of hamburgers, but for most of us, we just need to be known by a lot of people in a particular industry. Don't try to be Google or Hulu. Instead, aim to be the best and well known in a very specific and narrow market.

By narrowing your target market, you'll also be able to fine-tune your marketing and advertising messages. If you make watches, your advertising copy is going to be quite broad and varied. However, if you make watches for law enforcement officers and the watches have lights on them, are super durable, and include a lifetime warranty, you'll be able to create marketing copy that specifically addresses this audience. Language used to sell something or get someone to take action is often referred to as *copy*. *Content* is what you use to educate your audience, such as the content on your blog or the content of this book or the content written by an accountant to educate her customers on how to save money on their taxes.

Adam Bluestein writes on Inc.com[3] how Fun and Function, a company that makes items for special-needs children, had to radically change its marketing catalog. The catalog was designed for parents and spoke to them in a colloquial tone rather than a clinical tone, which is better suited for institutions. The biggest market for special-needs solutions are buyers such as hospitals and schools, not parents. Therefore, Fun and Function had to change its catalog to better communicate and speak to the customer base that was best for its business.

[3.] https://www.inc.com/magazine/201110/case-study-targeting-the-right-market.html

As you go narrow in a particular market, you become even more of a specialist. You get to know the market better, you speak the language, and you know the needs of that narrow market. I live in the New York City area; I can tell you how to get uptown and downtown, etc. However, someone who lives in Prospect Heights, Brooklyn, can tell you about a lot more streets and restaurants in that specific area of New York City. That person would be a specialist; I'm a generalist.

In 2014, I interviewed[4] business growth expert Casey Graham about this concept of going "niche." What he said back then is worth repeating now:

Niches are where the riches are—instead of marketing broadly and serving a large segment, focus on going more niche and more focused.

Dominate your market and nail it before you scale it—instead of adding more products and services, focus on dominating and adding value to a smaller market segment.

People will pay more than you think—if you offer intense value to your customers, they will pay a premium. If a customer spends $10,000 with you, ensure they get $50,000 (or whatever your numbers are) value from it.

---

[4] http://www.smallbiztechnology.com/archive/2014/03/why-hyper-niche-marketing-is-best-for-small-business-marketing-google-hangout-with-casey-graham-of-business-rocket.html/

Focus on Engagement, Not Followers or Likes

I catch myself glancing at how many followers I have on Twitter. As I write this I have about twenty-seven thousand followers. (By the way, do follow me @ramonray on Twitter!) Some days I look at my follower count and wish I had fifty thousand or five hundred thousand. I glance at how Gary Vaynerchuk gets eighty thousand likes on an Instagram post, and I'm happy if I get five or ten!

Sometimes we get caught up in the wrong numbers. How much do we weigh? How many calories did we consume? What's our annual revenue? What's our quarterly profit? How many parking tickets did we get? How many USB cables do we have? What numbers matter, and what numbers don't matter? If Joe, a technology consultant, has seven thousand LinkedIn followers and Steve, another technology consultant, has ninety-seven LinkedIn followers, this does mean *something*, right?

It is likely that Joe is doing something right in regard to sharing on LinkedIn and building a following. Still, it's important to remember to not get caught up in the numbers and not to obsess over follower count. It can be a dangerous obsession. Instead, focus on regularly educating your customers.

Steve, our tech guy with ninety-seven LinkedIn followers, should instead focus on providing great content to his followers, tagging relevant people, and using hashtags. Over time his follower count will grow, and people will begin to engage with him. By staying true to his core message—whatever that may be—his follower count will grow.

But more important than just the raw number of his

follower count are the **relevant** followers that "get" Steve's brand and his version of the world of tech. Those looking for expertise in technology consulting for their businesses will want to work with him. It's more important that among your followers on social media there are those who engage with you.

The New York Times wrote a substantive story[5] exposing how many celebrities feel so pressured to have a huge following that often they do the unthinkable: they buy followers. Don't do this; don't even think about it. Buying followers is not authentic. Often, they're not even interested in what you're sharing, and over time this will hurt your brand.

Having a large following is not the priority. What's important is having the right fans who are truly interested in what you have to say. If you educate and serve your customers, invariably you will get more followers, more engaged followers who will want to buy from you.

In fact, I'm getting comfortable with a smaller audience. Every time someone unsubscribes from my email newsletter, every time someone chooses to unsubscribe from me on Twitter, I'm happy. This is because I *only* want to share the "Ramon Ray" version of business growth with those who want it. I'm also excited because that means there's a higher percentage of people who want to hear from Ramon! It's a waste of *my* time and *their* time if I'm sending a message to people who aren't interested in it!

The real number you want to understand is the **level of engagement** people have with your content on social media. Sure, if you have ten million followers and 1 percent of them

---

[5.] https://www.nytimes.com/interactive/2018/01/27/technology/social-media-bots.html

buy your stuff, that's one hundred thousand buyers. Much better than having ten thousand followers and 1 percent of them buying your stuff. But this is rarely the case in business or in life.

Consider this: If you have five hundred followers who are maddeningly in love with your message and thus highly engaged with you, you'll have **a large engagement rate**. Maybe 30 percent of them will engage with you. That's a lot better off than five thousand followers who are just groupies, are really not all that in to you, and of whom probably even less than 1 percent engage with you in any meaningful way. Instead of seeking a huge number of fans (or followers), seek raving fans who are in *love* with your message and want to *engage* with you.

These are the people who will be paying more attention to your message, who will do what you ask them to do, and who will tell others about you. Stop looking over your shoulder while trying to catch up with the gal ahead of you or racing to stay ahead of the business that has just a few less followers than you.

Seek to do the best you can to provide **value** to your audience, to educate your tribe. Let it grow organically and passionately.

Joe Escobedo writes in *Forbes*:[6]

Engagement can tell you how well your content resonates with your audience. If your goal is to build a relationship

---

[6.]https://www.forbes.com/sites/joeescobedo/2017/06/12/social-media-engagement

with your audience, then you should definitely look at engagement. . . . That's why you need to look at not only your engagement but also your competitor's. By benchmarking their performance, you can determine which content resonates better—yours or your competitor's.

Jenn Deering Davis gives some advice on Union Metric's blog.[7] She shares:

The size of your audience on social media doesn't matter if no one is paying attention. In fact, we'll go so far as to say that how many followers you have doesn't really matter at all. So it's time to stop paying attention to your follower counts on social media and instead spend your time focusing what really matters—social media engagement.

While follower count does have some meaning, it is so much more meaningful to know *who* your followers are and how *engaged* they are. That's more important. Furthermore, work on getting followers who have influence. Who would you rather have: ten thousand fans who don't really care about your product or services, or one thousand fans who share your content with other people and comment and engage with you? Is this an audience who cares about your products, services, and solutions? Do you have followers who are rabid fans of the product or service you're selling? Focus on *who* is following you, not *how many* are following you.

---

[7] https://unionmetrics.com/blog/2016/05/engagement-vs-follower-count/

Engagement refers to the attention these followers will give you. If they are highly engaged followers, you will have much more of their attention. A few highly engaged followers are a lot more important and meaningful than a lot of followers who are not engaged or whose attention you don't have.

Influence—it's all about the engagement level and the type of people who are following those who follow you! There's another thing to remember: it's easy for people to follow you, to "like" you (as in a social platform). **However, when someone engages with your content it is a much stronger commitment and indication of your influence.**

The term *influencer*, which has gained popularity with the rise of social media, refers to an individual who has a community they influence. Maybe it's a fashion blogger who shares tips on casual business wear for men. He has a community that reposts, shares, and comments on what he publishes across social media platforms. This is engagement.

Also, engagement is more long term. If you just seek to "go viral," that's a flash in the pan, one-hit wonder. But if you seek for deeper engagement with your community, you are building a relationship that lasts.

Secret Sauce: Fans before Customers

As you seek to start and grow your personal brand and be a celebrity CEO, keep in mind the importance of building your base of **fans**, or as Ted Rubin[8] would say, **your community**.

Fans are not your customers. At least not yet. Fans are those people who have raised their hands, metaphorically, and said, "We like you," "We want to hear from you," "We enjoy being around you," "We like your content," etc.

[8] www.tedrubin.com

It's a challenge to sell to strangers. They don't know you. They're not sure they like you. In fact, you really don't know them. But it's so, so much easier to sell to fans. It's even easier to sell repeat products and services to fans.

As I travel around the United States and the world, I'm humbled and blessed by the fans who come up to me and say, "Ramon, I read your emails," or "Ramon, I love what you post on Facebook." Many of these have never bought anything from me, and that's okay. They do share my content, recommend me to others, and sometimes buy something from me.

I post quite a bit to Facebook, Twitter, LinkedIn, and Instagram. I also have an email newsletter and other channels. Through these channels and platforms, I've amassed a base of fans, people who have indicated in one way or another that they want to hear from Ramon. These include Hanna Perry,[9] owner of The Giggling Pig Art Studio; Adrian Miller,[10] owner of Adrian Miller Sales Training and Adrian's Network; Vikram Rajan,[11] founder of phoneBlogger.net and Videosocials.net; Beth Silver,[12] CMO for hire; Faith Kinslow,[13] branding consulting; Irina Smirnova, branding portrait photographer and speaker;[14] and so many others. These were all fans before they were customers. They signed up to my emails, liked my posts, commented on my videos, etc. Over the years when I've

[9] https://www.thegigglingpig.com/

[10] http://www.adriansnetwork.com

[11] https://phoneblogger.net/

[12] http://doubetllc.com

[13] http://www.trueidentitybranding.com/

[14] https://www.irinaleoni.com/

produced events or offered other things of value to them, they've become customers and bought something from me.

Instead of trying to find "a customer" to sell to, first offer value and seek to build a base of fans. If you build a base of fans, of people who know, like, and trust you, over time they'll buy from you again and again. When you build a base of fans, you've established trust. Trust is what makes influencers on social media so successful. Their communities trusts their opinions and recommendations.

Recently, I presented at an event about an hour away from my home. In the audience was one of my fans. She and a friend drove about ninety minutes to hear me speak that day. Why is this important? A follower will do the minimum to interact with you and your brand and your message. A fan will do much more, and this is what Seth is encouraging in his blog:

A blogger might convert 2% of readers to buy a book. (I'm aghast at this.) And a Twitter user with a lot of fans will be lucky to get one out of a thousand to click a link and buy something (.1%).

Likes, friendlies and hits are all fast-growing numbers that require little commitment. And commitment is the essence of conversion. The problem with commitment is that it's frightening (for both sides). And so it's easy to avoid. We just click and move on.

I think there's a transparent wall, an ever bigger one, between digital spectators and direct interaction or transaction. The faster the train is moving, the harder it is to pay attention, open the window and do business. If all you're doing is increasing the number of digital spectators to your work, you're unlikely to earn the conversion you deserve.

When you have a customer who buys from you, he or she is just a customer. It's transactional. When you have fans, they're lifelong customers and ambassadors for your brand.

Seth has launched a number of courses: altMBA, the Marketing Seminar, and the Bootstrappers Workshop. I signed up for the latter two courses. Thousands of people have each paid a few hundred dollars to a few thousand dollars for each of these courses. How did Seth do this? How did he essentially convince all of these people to purchase the courses he has offered? Because, over the years, he's built a fan base of highly engaged fans, people who read his blog (for free) and buy his books. The books are often twenty dollars or so each. Now that he has this fan base, he's able to monetize it even more by offering them something of even more value.

You can do this too. This is why building a base of dedicated fans is so important.

I spoke with Ted Rubin, a well-known social marketing strategist and keynote speaker, about his views on personal branding, and he said one of the most important things a business can do is to build a community instead of just building a network. If you build a community, or a fan base, you have strength, you have traction, you have people who will refer business to you and people who will tell others about you.

I'm not advocating that you get rid of your sales team or top sellers. Instead, I'm advocating that you start community building and fan building. It's ironic how fans and communities are something we use in the products-and-services world of business, but my guess is that it first became popular in the world of music.

With a music band, it's about having fans attending their concerts and buying their vinyl records, CDs, and, now, digital downloads.

Ditto Music helps bands distribute their music to various platforms, such as iTunes and Spotify. They wrote a blog post[15] giving advice to bands in how to build a large fan base. Coincidentally, most of the advice is appropriate for traditional business owners like you and me too.

1. Interact with your fans.

2. Play in smaller venues. (Remember we spoke about being a fish in a small pond!)

3. Hang around after gigs. (This is about engaging with your fans.)

4. Send exclusive emails. (Communicating with your fans and making them feel special is essential.)

5. Run competitions.

6. Give away free merchandise.

7. Share stories and insight in a blog.

[15.] https://www.dittomusic.com/blog/how-to-build-a-following-of-superfans

8. Showcase them in your music videos. (Promote your own fans and customers in your marketing!)

9. Create a unique bond.

Creating a fan base is NOT about selling to customers. It's about providing value to a community. It's about raising a flag that identifies who you are and what you stand for while giving your community and fans the opportunity to rally around you. Here's another perspective of fan building: we often ask for the "sale" too soon.

I'm advocating to seek fans *first*. Seek to build a community of people who are excited about you, who like you, who cheer you on. It's easier to get someone to clap for you and say "good job" or be appreciative of your work than to get a customer. As you build a fan base, you can then work toward converting fans to customers.

Let's pretend you're a local bookkeeper. Each week you put together events, volunteer at the local chamber, and help seniors better manage their money. You now have a fan base of people who know, like, and trust you. With a few purposeful inquiries you'll bubble up those who might *want to pay* for your services and hire you to help them. This has worked for me for over twenty years.

I don't need to sell or beg someone to buy from me. I have a growing fan base of admirers. The curious ones begin to ask me questions, then ask for a few minutes of my time, and they show further indications of interest than if I had given them a cold sales pitch. The next thing you know, I've just turned a fan into a paying customer. This powerful concept will transform your business.

I'm not advocating that you should not sell. Of course, you should sell. What I am advocating is that you focus your marketing energy on building a fan base and engagement. Selling will be much, much easier when you're working to convert a fan to a customer.

To build a fan base involves a long-view mind-set. The result does not come quickly; it's going take some time to plant the seeds to grow and attract an engaged audience.

Fans are comprised of just about anyone who likes someone. Being a fan does not mean you have to buy their products or their T-shirts or anything. Without fans, however, the next part of the equation will never happen, which is *customers*. Think about any good music band or performer. They have passive fans who may listen to them on the radio, active fans who follow all their interviews and announcements, and paying customers.

Customers come from fans who have such a desire for you that they want to take the next step and buy from you. Either they like what you have to offer and want it for themselves, or they like you so much they simply want to show their support. This is the power of being fan focused and not only sales focused.

An interesting twist on this aspect of fans (or followers) is a community member. Community members are even more engaged than fans. While fans want to get your email newsletter or attend a few events you may have, community members are all in. They want to wear your T-shirts, attend *every* event, put your stickers on their notebooks and computers, and more.

Melinda Emmerson, known as SmallBizLady on Twitter, interviewed IBM's social business manager, Alex de

Carvalho, for a Twitter Chat,[16] and he said that since people like to do business with companies they like, if you build a community, you can develop a group of customers and fans and bring them together into a community. This community will boost word-of-mouth referrals, encourage repeat visits, and more. People talking with other people about something they have in common builds engagement.

I didn't realize that I had a "community" until a few years into producing my Smart Hustle Small Business Conference. As I looked out at the attendees for the event, I started to cry. These were not just attendees buying a ticket. No, these were members of the Smart Hustle community. Throughout the day some people were tearing up with good emotions; some were screaming with excitement. Their emotional connection with the Ramon Ray, Celebrity CEO brand touched me as well. I bet you've been to a concert, church service, or other event where you could *feel* and *experience* the energy. This is the power of building a community (or fan base) and enabling them to get together in real life. You and your fans feed off of the energy of each other. Over time, with an email newsletter, a Facebook group, phone calls, and more, I built a community. You can do this too.

In the case of the Smart Hustle community, we are grouped by the type of businesses we run and how we run them. In your case, you could group people by geography, by common experience, or by a variety of things. However, I do believe that stronger communities are not grouped by demographics but by shared experiences and mind-sets.

Building, nurturing, and growing a community is not

[16.]https://succeedasyourownboss.com/
how-to-build-a-community-for-your-small-business/

easy. You'll need someone to be a community manager and be purposeful and tend your community, just like you would a wonderful garden in your backyard.

LOOK IN THE MIRROR: ARE YOU MAGNETIC?

One of the reasons, I'm told by clients, that they enjoy working with me is that I'm easy to work with. I've been told by clients that there are people they don't like working with because they're difficult to work with— prima donnas.

As you seek to build your personal brand, it's not just the "speeds and feeds" that are important, such as getting TV appearances or engaging on Twitter or speaking at events, it's also how you are as a person. If you don't have a magnetic personality that attracts people to you, if you're not likeable, it makes it so much harder to build a strong personal brand.

Here are some tips on being magnetic. While some of these may seem obvious to you, it's important to ground yourself in these tips to make an authentic impression:

1. **Smile!** A warm smile is inviting and such a fundamental human expression. Your smile can be seen and felt long before someone even shakes your hand.

2. **Have a great handshake.** A firm but not overpowering, full handshake is always appreciated. It speaks of confidence and feels great.

3. **Authenticity.** You can "smell" when you're talking with someone and he or she isn't interested in what you're saying. As you build your brand and

attract people to you, both online and in person, be authentic. Sure, you're going to be tired or not always feel chirpy, but you can always be polite and in the moment. People can tell when you're being a fake, phony fraud.

4. **Be a giver.** If you're always seeking to look out for YOU, your life will be self-centered. Instead, think of other people and how you can help them.

5. **Surround yourself with magnetic people.** Most of the people in my life are amazing and positive, and I enjoy being around them. Some of the people I get energy from are Yacov Wrocherinsky, Orion Global Solutions; Adrian Miller of Adrian's Network, and Vikram Rajan of phoneBlogger. net and recently Videosocials.net—these are my peeps!

6. **Feel great about yourself.** If you feel down and depressed, as I've struggled with in the past, you'll project this to other people. People who are magnetic have a confidence about them that they infect others with. One thing that everyone agrees on about President Barack Obama, whether you're a Republican or Democrat, liberal or conservative, is that he has a magnetic charisma about him—his smile, his handshake, his walk, his body language, and how he communicates.

7. **Be a good listener.** If you're always talking and seeking attention and not interested in what other people are saying, that's not good. Be in the moment, be appreciative, and be interested (or at least appear that way) in what other people are saying.

8. **Be humble.** It's ironic that I'm advocating you build your personal brand and promote yourself and also be humble. It's about promoting yourself, as you know you have something that other people need, but being humble enough to know you can learn from others and always appreciating others.

9. **Desire critique.** When I leave a stage, I often ask my clients and a few audience members what I can do to improve, how I can do better. The desire to do better is so important. We are not the best judge of ourselves; others are.

I think of my dear friend Shashi Bellamkonda, an early adopter of social media and content marketing. Over the years, he's shown me what a magnetic person is. When we've been together walking the halls of SXSW, for example, he knows everybody and everybody knows him. Shashi is a giver. He's always seeking ways to connect one person to another.

What about Phil Gerbyshak, a marketer, professional speaker, and social media consultant? Sure, he has a killer smile, but he's always in the mood for a big hug and a hearty laugh. You can feel Phil's warmth a mile away.

David Newman is another magnetic person. He's a trainer and consultant to some of the best speakers in the world. He hosts dinners and lunches for people at events. Sure, he's got a huge laugh and ready smile, but anyone who invites friends to dinner has to be magnetic.

Can shy people be magnetic? Someone who is naturally outgoing is going to have much more visibility and can quickly capture attention better than someone who is not. It's like having a flashing neon sign in Times Square versus a dim night-light in a dark room. Of course, the neon sign gets more attention.

However, if you're shy and more reserved, you can still have quiet magnetism. Your creative branding can still pop and stand out. When you *do* speak to someone, you can make that individual feel great and feel your energy, care, and concern. You might not get the instant attention of someone who is a bit louder and more outgoing, but you can still be magnetic in your own way, and most importantly, you can make a difference.

My wife and I speak together in public from time to time. She's shy (she says!) and doesn't readily go out of her way to shake a stranger's hand like I will. She'll probably never be the loudest person in a room. Although I have more humor and audience engagement, she's a much deeper and more thoughtful speaker than I am. Whereas I may speak for ten minutes on a topic and half the time people will be laughing, she'll speak for fifteen minutes on a topic and people will be taking notes and deeply hanging on to her every word.

There are many ways to be magnetic!

Does Physical Appearance Matter?

Let's digress for a minute and talk about how you *look*. I find that those with strong personal brands oftentimes, but not always, have a way they look that stands out!

If you Google "Ramon Ray" and observe how I've dressed over the years, you'll see three things that stand out:

1. I like to wear vests.

2. I love wearing bold ties and bold colors overall.

3. My socks are often brightly colored.

This is ME.

Your brand must be authentic. You should be true to who you really are; however, as you begin to build your personal brand, think about how you *look*. For good or for bad, how you look means something to other people. They form opinions about you just from how you look—BEFORE you even open your mouth.

If you're investing time and money into building your personal brand, it may be in your best interest to invest in the expertise of an image consultant who can guide you in how to look like the best version of yourself.

I happen to wear pocket squares with my suits, but maybe you wear a special tie clip with your suit. I prefer stylish brown shoes, while you may like wearing funky patterned socks that show your personality even when you're dressed for a business meeting. Whatever style you gravitate toward, try to aim to have a look that fits your personality but that looks sharp and polished.

Kimra Luna, personal branding and online business strategist, has blue hair. How many people do you see in business with colorful hair? She's definitely memorable. My friend Alfred Edmond Jr., executive editor-at-large for Black Enterprise, is known for his dapper suits, including his bow ties. Ted Rubin, digital strategist and speaker, is known for wearing snazzy vests and playful socks.

Jess Todtfeld, founder and president of the marketing training company Success in Media, dresses sharp and distinguished. His pocket squares and fitted suits look great. He credits our mutual friend Sylvie di Giusto for consulting him on how to enhance his public image.

While you don't *have* to dress fancy or interestingly, it helps to authentically stand out, every way you can.

3

Insight from Experts

CAROL ROTH, TV HOST AND AUTHOR

Years ago, before I knew what personal branding was, I had my eye on Carol Roth. Actually, I had my eye on her book about entrepreneurship. Carol is the founder of the Future File[17] legacy planning system, a TV and on-camera host, and the *New York Times* best-selling author of *The Entrepreneur Equation*. In an interview I had with her, she shared her insight on personal branding:

> *Personal branding is when you leverage your expertise and influence in a certain area, to further a personal and professional endeavor, in a consumer-facing way. Not only are you an expert in something but you've gained influence in your community, in front of your peers, to advance a particular business goal.*

---

[17] https://www.futurefile.com/

Carol's epiphany with personal branding came from her desire to scale her investment banking services and from seeing that so many business owners were getting bad advice. Most small business owners needed good financial advice, yet they often couldn't afford the retainer of an investment banker to get that advice. Carol saw an opportunity to help. Taking a page from personal finance guru Suze Orman, Carol launched her own journey to help small businesses with TV shows, products, thought leadership, and more. Today, Carol's pleased with how she's been able to help growing businesses! It's not been done exactly as Carol thought it would be, but nonetheless, Carol's vision of scaling herself has been achieved.

In your own business you have achieved some level of expertise. The key is to ensure your network is able to SEE that you have this expertise. You can show this if you've written books, or been featured on TV or other platforms that showcase your expertise. As Carol said, "Remember, people want to hire the person who wrote the book on a topic, not the one who read the book. People want to hire the person featured on TV, not the one who just watched TV!"

Know the importance of third-party credibility and how important it is for your personal brand. By creating a brand where you're highlighting your expertise, you can grow your business in an exponential way and crush your competition.

Carol does give one caution. When you're the face of your business and you have all the limelight, everyone wants to deal with you. Be sure you build in processes to scale your business beyond just yourself. As your business grows, have a plan to scale your business and transition so that your entire business is not running on just you.

In Carol's latest venture, Future File Legacy, a passion birthed from Carol's life experiences, more doors were opened because of her strong personal brand. Building your personal brand is an opportunity cost. For every TV show you go on and every interview you take, you are taking time away from doing something else. While going on TV can be an important part in getting the word out about your brand and building credibility, be sure you have a great team in place that can grow and manage your business as you take on this added task of being a celebrity CEO. Be prepared for the *time* you'll need to dedicate. But also be aware of the *success*—the new leads and customers and referrals—that will come as a result of your brand building.

Carol also advises that personal branding is not going to be appropriate for everyone. It's important to ask yourself if the ROI (return on investment) of personal branding makes sense for you and your business. I asked Carol if every business owner must leverage social media to harness their personal brand, and Carol said no. While for many businesses social media is best, it depends on your audience. For finance professionals they might do better speaking at big events and writing books.

However, if you're a business owner who makes lovely looking cupcakes, then Instagram may be perfect for you. In regard to social media, Carol advises that instead of trying to master every single platform, pick one or two and go deep. Master them and engage with your community!

JEFFREY HAYZLETT, SPEAKER, AUTHOR, AND FORMER FORTUNE 100 CMO

Jeffrey Hayzlett is tall and has a big laugh, a big smile, and a big personality. He's all about a BIG BRAND. I called up Jeff to get his insight into what it means to build a personal brand. He was blunt and to the point. For him, it's all about being the best—as he says, not being just good, but being GREAT.

Your brand is being built all the time. Other people are forming opinions about you, so you have no choice whether or not to brand. The question is, what is that brand? He explained that branding is not something you do, it's who you are. Branding is not about your logo or the warm-and-fuzzies of colors or fonts, it's about what promise you are delivering to your customers and those who are not yet your customers.

Jeff said that he's also in motion to reinvent himself; his brand is always evolving. Unfortunately, Jeff explained, a lot of people work more on what they look like instead of what they're trying to deliver. It's easier to dress up in a suit and look the part than to be the part and simply dress how you really want to dress.

So how do you build your personal brand?

1. Put a stake in the ground and declare what your brand promise is going to be; then . . .

2. Go do it. Walk it, talk it, and be it. You can't make it up or fake it; it's got to be real.

Jeff advises all professionals, especially those who are delivering a particular service (such as a speaker, author, or consultant), to spend time perfecting their craft. The more time you spend on your craft, skills, and knowledge, the better your brand will be.

If you're exceptionally good at what you do, other people will start talking about you; other people will start referring business to you. You'll be using other people's investments to build your brand and advance who you are.

JAY BAER, SPEAKER AND AUTHOR

Jay Baer[18] is one of the preeminent experts on all things marketing, customer service, digital marketing, and more. He's written a number of books that cover these topics. His latest book, *Talk Triggers*, is all about turning customers into brand evangelists. I figured if anyone knows about personal branding, it is Jay. Here's his advice.

As you start your personal brand you must be contextually appropriate. Meaning, if you're naturally a quiet and reserved person, don't try to be loud and energetic like Jay or Ramon may be. You be *you*.

Jay shares how the fast-food chain Wendy's Twitter personality is snarky and hip, but its retail store experience is not like that. Wendy's digital brand is not consistent with its in-person brand. Your personal brand should be consistent. Your audience can spot something that's not authentic and true.

He also says that it's important to ask yourself WHY you want to grow your personal brand. Just growing your personal brand for the sake of doing it is a waste of time. Know why you want to start and grow your personal brand.

In short, a strong personal brand builds trust, credibility, and visibility in the marketplace. Having trust and visibility

---

[18.] www.jaybaer.com

leads to more sales. If this sounds good to you, then go forth and seek to build your personal brand.

I asked Jay if every business must have a personal brand. He said that for professional services firms it's a must. If you're selling "time for dollars," for example, and not just selling a product, it's YOU who is the brand of your company. What you do is probably not so special, but who *you are* is special and should be amplified.

Speakers are a dime a dozen, but there are a few speakers, such as Ted Rubin, Jay Baer, Seth Godin, Guy Kawasaki, and Michael Hyatt, who have risen to the top. This is in part due to their personal brands.

Ironically, Jay struggles with thinking of having a personal brand. Heck, I know he does. He did tell me that whatever he does he wants to be sure that it's memorable, and he desires to treat everyone the same. Sure, Jay has an engine of content and education, but it's heartwarming to hear that those are his two principles of branding that he actively seeks to build on.

For me, social media is a massive part of starting and growing a personal brand and being a celebrity CEO. Jay's advice on this is, whatever you do socially, be consistent. How and what you post on Twitter should reflect how you speak in public.

For executives seeking to start and build their personal brands, Jay suggests putting together a list of what you're really passionate about. Put together another list of what you're an expert in. Using a Venn diagram, you should find an overlap of what you're passionate about and what you're the best expert in.

MICHAEL STELZNER, SOCIAL MEDIA EXAMINER FOUNDER

Social Media Examiner[19] is the leading company providing digital marketing insight and events for content marketing professionals. I asked its founder, Michael Stelzner, to share his insight on personal branding. His first question to me was, "Ramon, who do you think of when you think of video?" After about two seconds, I thought of Roberto Blake.[20] Why did he come to mind? Roberto has produced thousands of videos and generated millions of watch time for those videos. Roberto is the CEO and creative director of Create Awesome Media, LLC, and he is constantly educating his community, of which I'm a part, about video *through* video.

Michael said that providing value to your tribe is one of the essential elements to personal branding. One of the things people often do wrong is relying on one blip of success and not continuing to grow their personal brands. It's like trying to surf but not catching wave after wave. If you just catch one wave and ride it back to shore, you won't be surfing for long.

How do you succeed in personal branding? By identifying who you want to reach. Who is the ideal target audience? Understand what their needs are, and see what resonates and sticks with them. Look at the comments and analytics, and understand your tribe. Provide them with the education they need. Be relentless in providing insight and information and education to your audience.

Never, ever stop.

Once you get your *first* customer, don't stop there unless

[19.] http://www.socialmediaexaminer.com

[20.] http://www.robertoblake.com

you want a business that has only a few customers. But if you want to build your personal brand and be KNOWN, then seek to build your audience. Most of these people will not be your customers, but many of them will refer business to you. They'll provide you with free advertising. The creation of content is free marketing!

I asked Michael if we *have* to use social media and digital content. He said no. You can be a local musician, for example, and speak at local events, volunteer, etc. Over time you'll be known locally in your community. If you want to expand your brand, have it be more widely known, and build your fan base and market, then social media enables this to happen much faster—at scale.

Michael's a firm believer in podcasting as well. Interviewing experts in your industry gives you an affinity and social closeness to them, which enhances and builds YOUR brand. Podcasting is growing; people love to listen and be informed or entertained.

PART II

YOUR TOOLBOX

In the first part of *Celebrity CEO*, I've given you core concepts and principles to build your personal brand. In this second part I want to give you tools and show you how to use these tools to build your personal brand.

These tools and services will help you amplify and showcase your brand to the world. If you're the best veterinarian in San Mateo, California, but no one knows about it, you should be using Instagram to showcase the cute little animals you're helping. If you're the best violinist in Madrid, Spain, you should be using Facebook to showcase how your music changes lives. If you're the best accountant in Canton, Ohio, you need to use the power of LinkedIn to showcase your expertise by posting regular articles.

4

Website

Over the years I'm amazed at how many deals have come to me via my namesake website, RamonRay.com. I've gotten hired by billion-dollar brands, community colleges, and everything in between. Before people hire you, they're going to Google you (or "Bing" you!). Your corporate website is nice, and I bet it has information about your products and services, an "about" page, and other common elements. But to succeed at being a celebrity CEO, it's YOU whom they seek and want to get to know. Having a personal website, which focuses on YOU, will give possible customers a lot more focused information on who you are and why they should want to work with you.

A corporate website is a good start to host all the information about your company and its products and services. However, your personal website, your celebrity website, is equally important. It's all about *you* and your personal brand.

A website is a digital platform to give the world a chance to see you in the best light and to archive how amazing you are. Think of it as your digital storefront or office. You'll see on RamonRay.com that I have lots of visuals, both images and video. These are visuals I've collected over the years. Fans have sent them to me via social media, I've taken many of them, and I've used photographs from professionals I've hired.

Many people will "meet" you for the first time on your website or a social media platform. It is absolutely critical to build a professional, credible, and desirable visual in the mind's eye of the person seeking or discovering you online. The more and better images and videos you have about yourself, the better it helps someone make a decision to work with you.

Maybe you were mentioned in an article, or someone said how amazing you are, or someone saw you speak at an event. In all of these scenarios, people who want to work with you are still going to look you up and will, invariably, get to your personal website. You want them to see you in the best way.

Your celebrity website is where you list your accomplishments. This need not be like in a résumé you'd give to get a job. The purpose is to be a bit more conversational. In my case: *Ramon is an entrepreneur and best-selling author. He interviewed President Obama in the President's first live online video interview and got a selfie with Ivanka Trump by pitching her on his New York City roots.*

See how that snippet of my bio is conversational? You want to have a strong, powerful, and enticing bio on your website. Answer the questions the visitors to your website will ask: "Who are you?" and "Why should I care?"

It's also important to archive, or list, some of the great

media attention you garner. You'll see on RamonRay.com I have a page devoted to my TV appearances, interviews, and more.

Some people might argue that you don't need a website, that you all you need is a LinkedIn page or a Facebook page. I disagree.

When I tell people they can find out more about Ramon at RamonRay.com, it's much easier and more impressive than telling someone to look me up on LinkedIn or check me out on Facebook.

Here are a few elements to creating a great personal or celebrity website:

1. **Make it easy to get in touch with you.** Have your contact information readily available on your website. List your telephone number, or have an email address easy to see. The best option is a contact form. A website without contact information is a disservice to your website visitors. Why have a website if people can't get in touch with you?

2. **Easy to navigate:** No matter how simple or complex the content, make sure it is easy to navigate and get around. Your website need not be complicated or sophisticated. In fact, the simpler the better.

3. **Video:** Video is a great way to enable people to see you in action. Video humanizes and personalizes your brand. Make sure the video you showcase shows you at your best. I would

suggest having one or two quality videos on the front page of your website. These videos should give a summary of who you are, how you can help someone, and why they should care about working with you. Video is powerful and personal.

4. **Photos:** Action photos look great on your website. Use them strategically. Photos are a great way to give people a quick snapshot of who you are. While it may not be fair, people make judgements about working with you based on how you look. While some people opt to not use photos of themselves, I prefer you use a professionally created headshot of yourself, rather than a stock photo of a generic "business person."

5. **What's in it for me?** Clearly state who you are and why someone on your website might want to work with you. On your website, you need to QUICKLY capture someone's attention. To quickly explain HOW and WHY you can help them. It's important to remember WIIFM? **What's in it for me?** And *me* is your audience.

6. **Testimonials:** It's important to showcase what other people say about you through testimonials. If I'm a stranger and I don't know you, the best thing you can do is have others' testimonials about your service or their experiences working with you, prominently visible. Social media gives your

community the ability to praise you quickly and easily. I take posts from Twitter and embed them on my website. It's a quick, easy, and authentic testimonial.

7. **Call to action:** Have clear buttons or links so that people can take action. Do you want them to call you? Sign up for your email newsletter? Book you to speak? Get a free consultation? Put these on your website. People like and need direction; don't just write "80% of sinks get clogged by grease." But add "Download your FREE grease unclogging report here."

8. **Be mobile friendly!** It should look great on your cellphone. Many times, people just look at a website on their twenty-one-inch computer screen. It's important to also look at your website on a small smartphone screen. More and more people are going to use their smartphones, so ensuring the mobile experience looks good is essential.

9. **Security:** Your website shouldn't be a nesting place for hackers. Be sure that any forms, applications, or code is properly installed. Have your website audited by a security consultant to ensure it's as secure as possible against hackers.

My friend Dawnna St. Louis,[21] a top-selling author, entrepreneur, and speaker, coached me on some revisions for my website. Since her consultation it's been changed quite a bit, but her advice is still relevant. The copy (the words) on your website is so important. You should be using words that speak to who your ideal client is. If you're a graphic designer and want to help big clients, use words that speak to the results you can help them achieve. It's easy to get caught up in our own vanity, but instead focus on the customer and what their needs are and how you can convey this to them.

In case you're not sure how to build your website, here are some tips. There are two main ways you can build your website: You can do it yourself using "do it yourself" (DIY) website building tools such as Wix, Squarespace, or Weebly. Or you can hire a website developer to build one for you. They will most likely use WordPress and customize a template. You can also use a website designer that will build your website using a custom template from one of the DIY website services. There's no wrong way to get it done.

Hiring a web developer is going to be more expensive than doing it with a DIY website. If you decide to invest, there is the added benefit of a developer making the website customized to your needs, and you won't have to spend the time doing it. By doing it yourself, you'll save a lot of money and get your website done quickly. It's up to you to weigh the pros and cons that are right for you.

I built RamonRay.com using Wix, yet SmallBizTechnology.com and SmartHustle.com are hosted on WordPress and were built by my friends at Andio.com, professional website developers, founded by Andrew Schulkind. Part of

[21.] http://www.dawnna.com

having a great website is your domain name. Ideally you should use your name, like RamonRay.com. If you have a common name and it's taken, or if your name doesn't have a nice ring to it, then use something else. Example: JasonPiano.com or something like that works just fine. Get creative but keep it simple.

Picking a web host: If you use a DIY platform, that site will be your web host. If you choose to create your own website or hire a developer, you'll need to pick one of thousands of web hosts to host your website. Popular web hosts include GoDaddy and Network Solutions.

One more thing: if you want to blend a blog (which we'll talk about later) into your website, I highly suggest WordPress. It is one of the best tools for blogging.

5

Sales Funnels

Sales funnels are an important concept to understand. You can waste a lot of time with the "noise" of tweeting and posting on Facebook. You can attend endless network meetings. If you grasp the ever-important concept of your sales funnel, you'll have much more success in your business. You'll be able to convert the engagement on social media since it's now part of a strategy used to generate sales in your business.

It's so much easier to make money and generate sales if you have a pool of raving fans to market to. You're aware of the need to get those fans and followers to turn "likes" on a post and engaging with you into actually *buying* from you.

A **funnel** is a fancy way of saying that you are going to "touch" a prospective customer to move them along through a sales pitch disguised as a story or a scenario, or even a video, until they buy from you.

E. St. Elmo Lewis is credited with developing the components of a sales funnel that are used and referenced by most all marketers and sales professionals. His model is dated back to 1898 and is still relevant today. The steps are as follows:

Awareness—the customer is aware of the existence of a product or service

Interest—actively expressing an interest in a product group

Desire—aspiring to a particular brand or product

Action—taking the next step toward purchasing the chosen product

William Townsend is credited with mapping these steps into an actual funnel. Over the years various experts have modified and expanded on this funnel, but the concepts are all the same. It's about touching the customer, educating the customer, and guiding them toward taking action to buy from you.

Touching the customer means sending the prospective customer an email newsletter, giving him a call, inviting him to an event—anything you can do to remind him that you have a solution for his needs. You do this most effectively by regularly sending information of VALUE to him.

Instead of always having to buy the attention of someone from someone else—that's advertising—you can work on getting your own fan base to buy from you through your sales funnel. A sales funnel is a description of the journey a *potential* customer goes through to become an *actual* customer.

If you know this journey for your products and services, you'll be successful.

Here's a typical sales funnel:

You have the **top** of the funnel. These are potential customers who don't know you. They're not familiar with your brand or what you do. Due to some action you did to get their attention, they've connected with you in some way. Maybe they saw a tweet you did and followed you; maybe they came to an event where you spoke; maybe they met you at a networking event. These are folks at the top of your funnel. We will call them your baby fans.

The **middle** of the funnel is made up of those who now know who you are and are starting to interact with you. Maybe they've attended two or three webinars you conducted; maybe they've downloaded a PDF. These are folks who are interested in what you're saying (or selling). They are being educated through the content you're providing them. This interaction furthers them on the journey of liking and trusting you.

The third part of the funnel is the **bottom** of the funnel. These are the folks who are HOT and ready to buy. The simple question is, will they buy from *you* or from someone else? Or even better, are they buying from you today or tomorrow? The bottom of the funnel, or "almost customers," don't need much more education, they just need to be guided into why you, your company, and your product are the best choice for them, and be triggered into actually buying from you. Here's when you make them the offer to buy!

Things like the design of your shopping cart (for those selling online) or how you ask for business during a phone call can make or break a sale for those at the bottom-of-the-funnel stage. That is one aspect of the sales funnel.

The other aspect of the funnel is knowing *your funnel* for your particular industry and specific business. What's the sales funnel of *your customers?* Once you get a fan, how do you convert her to a customer?

A car dealer selling a $90,000 Maserati has a different type of sales funnel than a web designer selling her services to dentists. The car dealer's sales funnel might include a test drive, an in-home consultation, and so much more. Maybe it takes six months to a year. A web designer's sales funnel might include a series of ten emails and a consultation via webinar.

You'll notice that a sales funnel is often about education. It's about trust. Your goal is to continue to offer *value* to your fans and to make offers to a subset of those fans in order to draw them deeper into a particular funnel.

For example, let's say your goal is to get more logo design clients in Atlanta. Your first step would be to post on LinkedIn something like this: "Do you live in Atlanta? Want a better logo? Join our free webinar with tips on what makes a great logo." For those who attend the webinar, you might then offer to give them a free audit of their existing logos.

From those who take you up on your offer for a logo audit, you can then find out who might want to pay $999 to have their logos redesigned. This is a very simple example, but it shows the reason and the power of turning a fan into a customer. Know your sales funnel.

Mark Swallows, a writer for Fit Small Business, writes in a blog post[22] of the power of a well-constructed sales funnel. He tells us to be very purposeful and clear in how our customers buy from us. It's also essential that our customer

22. https://fitsmallbusiness.com/sales-funnel/

touch points (this includes sales, marketing, and customer service) all have a common methodology in how they communicate with customers. Finally, if we have a well-developed sales funnel, we'll be able to forecast and predict the ebb and flow and our sales cycle.

Rarely will someone buy from you the first time they interact with your brand. It often takes several interactions before they buy—hence the power and purpose of your sales funnel. Since it takes multiple interactions to get someone to buy from you, a sales funnel disciplines you to make those multiple interactions with interested prospective customers.

Seth Godin wrote about the sales funnel in a 2006 blog post.[23] It particularly relates to people using Google to search for information:

Once you see the funnel, it's easy to understand how valuable your existing customers are, and easy to think about how you want to spend time and money in promoting and building your site. Most marketers are running a flat campaign. Embracing the funnel changes the way you treat people. And treating different people differently is what consumers demand.

You'll see in later chapters of the book that I write about the specific tools I use to build my personal brand. It's not using *one* particular tool; it's about using a variety of tools (and services) to touch your fan base on a consistent basis so you're always top of mind. Your marketing strategy for

---

[23] https://seths.blog/2006/01/understanding_t-2/

building your personal brand won't be complete just by tweeting. That's a big part of it, but it's the full spectrum of a tweet (which could be the tip of the engagement iceberg) to having someone sign up for your email newsletter (which gets them a bit deeper into your awareness orbit) to having them attend an event (which gets them even further into your orbit where now maybe they're a fan) to them being interested in having a phone call with you (now they're *really, really* interested in what you have to offer) to them buying from you.

This is exactly how the marketing for my business works quite successfully. I post quite a bit on a variety of social platforms. I also send out a regular email newsletter. Not only do I speak at many events, but I produce my own events as well, such as the Smart Hustle Small Business Conference.[24]

This "circle of attention" for my fans leads to customers (mostly large brands) finding me and asking me to work with them. This works for me and it can work for you, in any industry.

Some people tease me for the massive amounts of content I post online, particularly in my videos. I often do Instagram and Facebook stories, post videos with insight on business topics, share videos of myself cutting and eating fruit . . . you get the point.

But this works.

While I have a fan base and community of thousands of followers, including small business owners, my revenue and my paying clients are the larger brands. These larger brands specialize in selling to small business owners. The reason my business is so successful is because I'm always top of mind in

[24.] http://www.smarthustle.com/conference

these brands when they're considering a new campaign to reach their small-business customers.

It's *my* funnel. Not as in depth or extensive as a funnel by a traditional sales person selling lights to a university, but it is a funnel. Through my videos and overall content, I'm ensuring that the fifty to one hundred brands that might want to work with me are constantly moving from the top of the funnel (creating awareness and interest) toward the bottom of the funnel (where they're customers or seriously considering working with me).

Build a sales funnel to be top of mind and touch your fans, as well as potential and actual customers, all the time.

6

Social Media

There are ten zillion books on social media. Go read them. Randomly pick any of the top ten books on Amazon and you'll get up to speed on the basics of how to use social media. I recommend books by Chris Brogan, Michael Hyatt, Guy Kawasaki, Ann Handley, Gary Vaynerchuk, and a few others. Understand, no matter how much you try, you're not going to be able to keep up with every trend, algorithm change, and feature of the social media platforms. Who knows?—by the time you read this, maybe Facebook will have shut down and LinkedIn will be a distant memory. Highly doubtful, but you get my point! Don't focus so much on the itty-bitty details of social media, but focus on the BIG picture.

What I'm going to do in this section is give you my tips for how I use social media to build my celebrity status. Social media is POWERFUL. In fact, it is one of the most powerful ways to get attention and keep attention. Visit any of my social media profiles and you'll see I'm always posting something. My main platforms are LinkedIn, Twitter, and Facebook. Maybe for you it's Twitter and Instagram.

A question I'm often asked is, "Ramon, which platform should I choose?" The right platform is the one you feel most comfortable with and the platform where your tribe thrives. In my case, my community, my tribe, is not on Snapchat, so I don't use it. They're also not on Pinterest, so I don't use it. Here's my simple yet very effective method for using social media: Frequency, Relevancy, Engagement, Analytics— FREA.

FREQUENCY

It is essential to post on social media with *frequency*. Does this mean to post on Facebook every hour on the hour? Of course not. That's too much for Facebook. Does it mean to post to Twitter every three minutes? No. Unless you're covering a breaking news story with minute-by-minute updates, it's overkill.

Keep in mind, on social media, the platform is like a moving stream of water. You tweet at 8:00 a.m., and hours later it's unlikely your tweet is going to be seen by very many people as the thousands of other Twitter users push your 8:00 a.m. tweet down the feed. Of course, those following you closely or those closely following a hashtag will see it, but most people will not. So frequency is important.

Here is my guide—and it's only a guide:

- Post on Twitter several times a day with content (good content) spaced out over time.

- Post on Instagram and Facebook no more than three times a day. More than that and you might annoy people.

- Post on LinkedIn once a day, maybe even once every other day.

You've probably heard the axiom "out of sight, out of mind." This is very true when using social media. There are millions of conversations happening on all the platforms. There are thousands of conversations happening on any particular topic. If you want to be top of mind to your fans, to your community, frequency is important.

I've started using Instagram and Facebook stories a lot more, to add even more content to my social feed. With a "story," you won't clutter and crowd the news feeds of your fans. If they're interested in you, they have the option to click on your story to see every detail that you wish to share with them. You can do five stories in an hour, and that's okay. But don't post five times on Facebook in an hour; that can be annoying and cause people to stop following you.

RELEVANCY

Being relevant to your audience is vital to establishing a tribe. My wife, Ronnie, was a homeschool mom. We've now fully "graduated." Today she spends some of her time educating other moms about homeschooling and more. She's highly relevant and focused on her community and tribe. This relevancy has caused her followers and overall engagement to increase.

We talked about engagement earlier in the book, right?

My wife has a high engagement rate. She doesn't have a lot of followers, but a high percentage of them engage with her posts.

If you're not relevant to your community, they'll simply stop following you or, even worse, stop paying attention to you. Always seek to be relevant to your audience, and share content with them that's important to them.

What's going to make them laugh? What's going to educate them? What's going to make them smarter? What do you have to offer that will help THEM? Focus on their needs, and use your professional expertise to stay highly relevant to what is important to them. Figure out what your tribe wants to know about, then be true to that, *feed* it to them, and you will hold their attention.

Can you, once in a while, post about your family vacation or show yourself doing something fun on the weekend? Sure! In fact, it's great to get a little personal and have fun with your content, but don't let content that is NOT relevant to your audience be what's most important.

If you are not sure what to post, here are a few ideas for inspiration:

1. **Ask a relevant question.** If you have a veterinary clinic, you might post cute pet photos and ask your followers to vote on which one they like best. Asking questions is a great way to build engagement.

2. **Leverage important dates.** During the holidays, share holiday-themed content and ask holiday-themed questions. If you're a sales consultant,

why not count down the days to Christmas with one sales tip a day?

3. **Highlight your customers.** Interview a customer and share his or her story or insight with your audience. People love being promoted and love sharing, and they love hearing from other people.

4. **Answer questions.** What are the top questions your community wants answered? Answer those questions.

5. **Reading lists.** People love to read and get smarter. Put together a reading list of books or other content (e.g., blog posts).

6. **Understand your reader.** As you're writing content, write it with your reader in mind, not with yourself in mind.

7. **Use keywords and SEO.** Whether posting to a social media platform or to a blog, use keywords in your title and in the copy. People are SEARCHING for your insight; be sure they can find it.

People who are not clear on their message and who their audience is will post the least relevant things. The more focused you are on sharing content that your audience will appreciate and like and NEED, the more engagement and interest your audience will have.

ENGAGEMENT

Engaging content that captures attention is essential. It's called "social media" for a reason. The *media* is the photos, videos, and audio that you share with your tribe. This imagery should cause people to stop scrolling and should capture their attention. It could be as simple as a photo of you speaking at a conference with the word "WOW" superimposed over the photo. It could be a photo of you holding up your index finger, indicating "one," with an accompanying post about the power of one small step.

You can even have engaging content with no media. Sometimes I post with JUST text. But when I do it, I do it like this: "Why Are You Satisfied? Last week I was taking my daughter to school and saw someone . . ." See how I started the post with a question that is sure to catch attention? No image, but it's still an *engaging* post.

Some traits of an engaging post include the following:

- A bold visual image

- Text on an image

- A call to action; use words in your content that tell people what to do.

- Not boring.

- Doesn't use lots of dense text; people want to skim and then click for more information.

- A catchy headline

Content that's engaging catches the eye. It's so powerful that people want to share it with others. It's bold and screams for attention and action. You don't have to create every bit of content; you can also curate great content and share it with others. Think about news.google.com—there's not one bit of "news" on there that Google creates, yet it's a popular destination.

Engaging content takes many shapes and forms. It's not "just a blog" post, but content that includes podcasts, memes, videos, images, lists, and surveys in addition to blog posts. If you make a video, you can convert the audio from that video into a podcast, turn that podcast into a blog post, create a few images around the content, and more!

I'm always on the lookout for engaging content that will illustrate something. Organic (natural) content, infused with a message is a WIN. As I type this text, here's a list of the imagery I observed just in the past few hours:

- A loyal dog sitting in its master's lap while he checks his email

- Railroad crossing sign—, blaring horn and lights blinking

- My room at the Ace Hotel—eclectic! It even has a record player.

These are just three of the engaging images I've seen in the few hours I've been awake. Be observant, and use the world for inspiration. Part of capturing engaging imagery is just to be *aware* of your surroundings and not keep your head down!

ANALYTICS

Measure what you're doing. On a regular basis check your social media statistics to see which content performs best, what times your audience is most engaged, and the demographics of your audience. If you use a tool such as Buffer or CoSchedule, it's great for seeing statistics on your social content. You can also use Google analytics to check the traffic of your website—what pages are read the most, who is referring content to you, and more. Many of the business versions of the social platforms have analytics built into their platforms.

I can use Buffer, for example, to see which content was most popular over the past seven days. I also use AddThis to enable my audience to share content from my websites. AddThis also provides analytics so I can see which content was most popular with my audience.

You don't want to post content just for the sake of posting content, but you want to post content that resonates most powerfully with your audience. Understand what content is most popular. Some things will trigger your audience to take action and some things won't. Use analytics to *listen* to your audience and provide them with the content they want.

I post lots of video on Facebook, and using Facebook analytics I can see which posts, which contained video had the most views. That's the FREA concept.

Frequency. Relevancy. Engagement. Analytics.

Try it. You'll like it, and you'll see it give a dramatic boost to your personal brand.

LINKEDIN

LinkedIn is currently the most powerful platform for connecting with other business owners. You won't find kids on there. You won't find grandparents sharing photos of their newest grandchild. You won't find middle-aged women sharing their baking secrets. Nope, you'll find people who are in **business** and want to connect about **business**.

While LinkedIn is a powerful way to connect one-on-one with a particular professional you want to meet, it's so much more. I use LinkedIn to post substantive educational content. I don't post updates about what I ate (I do that on Facebook and Instagram from time to time). Instead, I post videos giving business insight to my community, or I might pose a question to be answered to engage with my following.

You'll notice that LinkedIn is encouraging people to use hashtags. This is a relatively new and good thing. Hashtags let people find specific content on LinkedIn and the other platforms as well. While YouTube and, more recently, Facebook are leaders in video content, I've found that LinkedIn is becoming an oasis for good, quality, business-focused video content.

Beth Granger is a personal friend, and she is a LinkedIn and social media consultant. I asked her to share her best tips for using LinkedIn as a platform for your personal brand.

1. **Use a professional upper-body photo.** Beth's tip: *No one likes their photo; get over it. Really. No one wants to do business with an "empty head" icon. You need a professional image. Please don't use a photo from vacation with the people next to you cut off.*

Too many times I've seen professionals include photos of their kids and spouses in their profile photos. Don't do this unless it's directly relevant to your business. Instead, use a professionally taken or at least high-quality photo that helps you look your best. Remember, people form opinions about you based on how you look. If you're a web developer, let people focus on YOU as a professional. Using a blurry photo of yourself and your three nephews distracts me from considering YOU.

2. **Use a background image.** Beth's tip: *Making a background image will set you apart. Think of it as your personal/professional billboard.*

   You can use a nice action image as your background. Use something exciting, not boring. This is your "hero" image that people will quickly glance at, but it will make a positive impact in people looking further at your profile.

3. **Think of your headline (the text under your name) as your 120-character elevator speech.** Beth's tip: *By default, your headline will be your job title, but don't waste this space. Use it to start telling your story. It can be a single statement or multiple keywords and phrases. The format that works for many people is "I work with [insert your ideal client or industry] to [what do you do for them?]." Do include the keywords that apply to you.*

Remember, the person looking at you on LinkedIn is probably quickly browsing on his cell phone and has a short attention span. Your headline is that snippet that encapsulates who you are in a short statement. Be thoughtful about what you put here. In some of my bios, I weave in my love of burnt pancakes and bacon AND that I'm a global keynote speaker. Yep, it sounds kind of corny, but this headline stops people scrolling and gets them to take notice long enough that they want more information to consider working with me.

4. **Your summary is what you say when someone says, "Tell me more."** Beth's tip: *Your summary is the place to tell your story, express your passion for what you do, and be findable for appropriate keywords. Do write it in first person. This is not your third-person bio.*

When we write summaries about ourselves, we often think only of *ourselves*. While Beth guides us to write from the first-person perspective, I suggest trying a different approach by breaking this rule. Even in my posts on Facebook, I often use third-person perspective. Such as "Ramon is looking to hire . . ." or "Ramon learned this important lesson . . ." Why? I find that third-person captures more attention. The person reading it will know what the forthcoming information is about. Also keep in mind that you don't have to use a full, grammatically correct sentence. It's okay to write something like "Lawyer for startups. Ramon helps high-growth companies scale."

5. **Write articles and post status updates about relevant topics.** Beth's tip: *You will get good exposure with your connections and their connections (your second connections) by writing articles and status updates that highlight your expertise. Also, your articles and updates will show up on your profile. Again, real estate you control!*

Blogging used to mean creating a WordPress website and adding content on a regular basis. While blogging still means frequently updating content, you can blog from anywhere. Regularly posting content on LinkedIn is a form of blogging. Sure, it might not be indexed by Google, but you can repost it to another platform. Articles on LinkedIn are often longer and more substantive. Post or updates should be shorter and more to the point.

6. **Video is powerful on LinkedIn.** My advice: More business professionals are using LinkedIn for more than simply connecting with other people. They are using it to educate themselves and learn about their industries. This is a perfect opportunity for you. As I've said before, video is a way to humanize and personalize your brand. Using video on LinkedIn brings this experience to a community of B2B professionals. Video on

LinkedIn should be of higher quality than what
might be appropriate on Facebook or Twitter.
These videos should have great lighting and
audio, and even use captions so that people can
watch your video with the audio off.

TWITTER

I love using Twitter. It's a great platform for microblogging.
It's also the only platform where it's acceptable to post five
to ten times a day. Since Twitter is a steady stream of short
nuggets, you pretty much *have* to post several times a day.
If you post something at 8:00 a.m., only a small percentage
of your community will see it throughout the day. Posting
often is a good thing so long as your content is engaging and
useful for your audience.

On Twitter you don't have to post only original insight,
you can retweet (RT) great posts from other people. Some
people have been quite successful by sharing or retweeting
other people's content along with their own original posts.
Liking and re-sharing can be just as important as posting
original content.

Here are two ways I use Twitter to polish my personal
brand and gain visibility in front of my core community:

1.   Take part in popular, trending hashtags or
     keywords. For example, on Sunday mornings
     one of the most popular hashtags is in fact
     #SundayMorning. I will post something with this
     hashtag and ride the wave of its trending. Even
     though it will not be trending all day, I participate
     while there are millions of people following

that hashtag. In doing this, I get just a bit more visibility than I normally would.

2. Participate in Twitter chats. Twitter chats are real-time communications using an agreed-upon hashtag. Buffer has a chat every Wednesday at 10 a.m. EST—follow the hashtag #BufferChat, for example. By participating in Twitter chats you'll learn and also be able to share your knowledge with others.

Sara Wolkiewicz, writing for Mention.com,[25] gives five pointers on using Twitter for brand building.

1. Choose your Twitter handle carefully.

2. Choose your brand's imaging.

3. Find your brand's voice.

4. Start building connections and influence.

5. Become a master tweeter.

I've been using Twitter since 2007. For most of you reading this book, that's a long time. Here are a few things I've learned from my Twitter years. Your profile matters. Be sure to have a profile image or photo and a header image that can capture attention and best represent you.

I change my images every so often to keep things fresh.

---

[25] https://mention.com/blog/twitter-personal-branding/

After I speak at an event, invariably there are a few photos of me. If the pictures are awesome, I use them. Have you been to an event or an experience where they offered free headshots? This is a great opportunity to get a nice new set of photos for Twitter and other platforms.

While you're analyzing your profile, give some thought to your profile description. Roberto Blake puts hashtags (I use #CelebrityCEO, for example) in his Twitter description. The purpose is for people who are searching for this hashtag to discover him.

The handle you use to define yourself on Twitter is important. I'm pretty happy with @ramonray. I know some people have all sorts of things—@Jenny587girl or @SurferDude87. These are okay for the everyday person. For business purposes, though, you should have a Twitter handle that best reflects your personal brand. If you have invested a lot of time into building a nondescriptive Twitter handle, you'll probably want to keep it. If you are just starting out, see if you can get one that is more descriptive of who you are today *or* who you want to be.

Now that you've set up your Twitter profile, let's think about your day-to-day usage of Twitter. It's important to follow people or brands that you are most interested in. You want to do this so you keep up to speed with what interests you. You will also find content to share with your own Twitter followers and begin engaging with others who can promote *your* content and brand.

On Twitter you can build curated lists of other Twitter users, so you can more easily and quickly keep up to date with their content. These are called Twitter lists. I have a few lists for news, another for all things small business, one for various small-business journalists, and more.

I have also found using Twitter mobile notifications very useful. While I can't keep up with the steady stream of tweets coming through my Twitter news feed, I am notified each time certain people tweet. I do this to keep up to date on what's important to them and so I can retweet and comment on their posts. This is what social engagement is all about. When *you* engage with others it encourages *them* to engage with you.

There's no perfect way to create content on Twitter. But here are a few things you want to consider. It's what I do!

- **Retweet**—I actively look for great content from other Twitter users that might be of interest to my audience that I can share with them.

- **Comment**—I always look for ways not to just retweet but also to comment on the tweets of others. This is an even *more* purposeful engagement.

- **Fresh content**—Every Friday, I go through my email newsletters and go to online articles, which I can schedule to share on my Twitter feed as well. I use Buffer to help me schedule social media shares. By doing this, I'm keeping a steady flow of great content of interest to my community going through my Twitter feed. Imagine turning on the TV or going to Hulu or Netflix and not seeing fresh content! You'd quickly stop checking them out. Your Twitter feed, and that of other social networks, is no different.

I find that with Twitter I can post as frequently as I want and people don't mind. People expect a steady flow of content through their Twitter feeds, as opposed to Facebook, where they don't want a steady flow of updates about your life. So on Twitter you can post several times a day if the content you are sharing is of value to your community.

Sometimes I post on Twitter several times an hour or minute! When? During conferences I "live tweet" the presentations. My audience and community love this. They can't be there, but appreciate the live updates I share during the event.

When live tweeting an event, here are a few things I do, which also work well when sharing live updates from an event:

- **Liberal tagging**—Be sure to tag others. We all have some measure of vanity about us, and everyone appreciates knowing that someone is mentioning them in a tweet. Only tag those who are relevant to the tweet you are posting.

- **Hashtags**—Especially during events or particular campaigns, use a hashtag so that others at the event or associated with the campaign can follow along and see what you're sharing about the event or experience. Instead of watching TV together, you're enjoying and learning about the experience together.

- **Selfies**—I love taking selfies at events and all other occasions. At events, selfies are especially nice, as everyone's attention is focused around a common theme. So take a selfie, tag those in the selfie, and use the event hashtag.

PHOTO TIP: When taking photos, hold your camera at an angle a bit higher than everyone's heads. It's more flattering to many people. There are no double chins or other things that many people might not like.

Twitter is, like all other platforms, very image friendly. It's great to take an interesting picture and share it on Twitter with related content or information. For example, don't just take a photo of yourself standing in front of a wall. Maybe hold the camera at a slight angle with a nice picture or other image behind you. It makes a less boring background and one that's more eye catching.

Video, of course, is powerful on Twitter as well. At events, I often take a short (two minutes or less) video of the presenter and share that with a quote about what he or she said. Try to anticipate what the person is going to say so you can capture a nice nugget of his or her thoughts. Part of using Twitter successfully is just sharing great content. It's also about sharing other people's content and tagging them.

Here is another Twitter tip: ASK. From time to time I email friends (or direct message them on Twitter) and ask them to retweet something I've tweeted. If you're promoting something new, like a product, book, new service, or even a fresh blog post, you can do this. Don't do this a lot, but from time to time it's okay, especially if you've been very giving and have shared their content as well.

Instagram

Instagram is powerful, and it is growing. While every social media platform is best optimized by posting engaging content with either video or images, on Instagram it is a MUST.

I find that my biggest success in using Instagram comes from using hashtags. People are actively searching to connect with other people's profiles on Instagram, and hashtags are how they do it. When you post, be sure to use relevant hashtags. On all platforms you can use hashtags to help people easily find the keywords you're posting about. However, I find that on Instagram (and Twitter) hashtag use is much more popular than on Facebook or LinkedIn.

Since Instagram is first and foremost a visual platform, should you create a short video with great content that's fun and engaging? Yes. Should you post an image with text overlaid on the image? Yes. There are so many tools and apps you can use to edit your images and videos. I use an app to add text over my pictures before posting.

Instagram is all about "vertical" content. When you take videos that you want to share on Instagram, your camera must be vertical. This platform is primarily viewed on mobile devices, so content is created to fit an upright phone screen.

Before you use Instagram, and this is my advice for *all* platforms, be sure you know what platform your audience is on. If you're not sure, for a few days post actively on all the major platforms. See where you get the most response. This is how you'll know which platform or platforms to focus on. You need not be on all platforms, but at least focus on two.

Instagram has a "business account" option that has added features beyond a regular Instagram account. While you'll get far by just using a personal Instagram account, you'll find that you can enhance the audience-engagement features and other cool options with a business account. In particular, you will have access to insight, statistics, and analytics.

Instagram stories are *very* popular. As you build a strong community, they will want to hear more and more from you, and for whatever reason, they'll be interested in your day-to-day activities. Stories enable you to be authentic, or "real." You can give people a peek inside what's happening "now" or "today." I've found that, with stories, community members (fans!) who are extremely interested in you can follow you up close and a bit more personally.

Think about the celebrities you follow online. Notice how many people like to know what they cooked, where they went shopping, and what their days were like. As a celebrity CEO, your fans are interested in you too. I don't document my entire life on Instagram. When I'm out and about, maybe at an event or travelling, I use Instagram stories (which I share to Facebook stories via the Instagram app) as a way to share about the day-to-day portion of my life.

For example, maybe I'm getting into an Uber or just leaving an event. I'll use Instagram stories to share some quick insight with my community. I'm not clogging up their feeds, and I know that only the most interested fans will click the icon to see what's going on in my world.

FACEBOOK

Facebook is the mother of all social media platforms. It's the biggest, most popular, and most used platform as of today. How can you leverage its power to your benefit to build and boost your personal brand?

By simply posting great content that is engaging and relevant on a regular basis, you'll be on the right path. You can take things up a notch by using video. Facebook (along with other platforms) loves video. Don't link to videos that are on YouTube or any other platform. Instead, upload the videos directly to Facebook. This is called natively using the app. Let's say you're at a client's office and you do a three-minute video interview with her about how she's using your product to help solve a problem in her business. Your first inclination might be to upload it to YouTube. Great. Upload it to You-Tube and add descriptive remarks in the description, using keywords in the description and the video title. In addition, take the video and upload it directly to Facebook. Consider creating a shorter version, about 120 seconds, and sharing it on Twitter by uploading it directly to Twitter through the app. Platforms are selfish. They give more weight to video that's uploaded directly to their platforms than shared via other platforms.

Live video is very popular on Facebook. If you do use live video, let your audience know ahead of time—schedule it. Use it as a way to answer questions, to get feedback, and to showcase yourself while shining the light on your fans.

Facebook Groups are very popular and are an easy way to build engagement with your fan base. A Facebook Group is like a club; use it to share special offers or news with your raving fans. Successful groups have clear rules of engagement. For my Smart Hustle Community Group, the rule is that you can only ask a question about your business. I don't allow promotion or advice, for the most part; just a simple question. I also moderate each post to be sure this rule is followed.

Your group might be different. I'm a member of a group where there is no moderation, but all the members are thoughtful about what they post.

A group such as the National Speakers Association, with thousands of members, is moderated. When someone posts in the group, it can take a few hours or more than a day for it to be approved and to go live in the group.

A Facebook group is a great way to enable your fan base to have discussions around your brand and what your brand services. Let's say you're a fashion consultant. Your Facebook Group needs not be all about *your* consulting, but it can be about all things fashion.

As your community grows, you'll get more and more comments. Respond to these comments, and other user actions, as best you can. Facebook's design encourages lots of comments, messenger chats, replies, and more. Be sure that YOU are engaging on Facebook (and all social platforms). If people ask you a question, respond. If someone critiques or compliments you in a post, respond positively and constructively.

Remember as a celebrity CEO, part of the way you build your community is to **respond** to your community. If you feel you won't have time for your community, it might be best to not create a community. Imagine inviting people to your birthday party and when they come, you don't show up, or you ask them not to sing "Happy Birthday!"

TIPS FOR EVERY SOCIAL PLATFORM

Here's a summary of tips for every social platform:

- Your profile: fill it out as completely as you can, and keep it interesting.

- Your image: have your profile images looking nice and sharp. Look your best.

- Follow relevant people: follow or like people and brands relevant to your industry.

- Tag relevant people: tag people and brands relevant to the content you're posting and to your industry.

- Share great content: always think of others when you're sharing content, and ask "Is this useful to them?"

- Don't follow everyone who follows you: you don't have to follow everyone who follows you or like every page or comment. It's okay to have 5,171 people following you and you only follow 175 people who are meaningful to you.

I hear over and over and over again, "Ramon, you are *everywhere.*" These people are not complaining, but are complimenting me on how they've seen a rise in my "celebrity status" online. Of course, I'm not literally everywhere, but it sure does seem that way. Since I post a lot of content on a variety of platforms, and other people tag and reference me and I tag and reference other people, the illusion of Ramon being everywhere is created.

As you seek to be a celebrity CEO, steal a few tips from my playbook and you'll be seen as being everywhere by your fans as well.

7

Blogging

I'm a firm believer in the power of blogging. I first started my blog using desktop software—shocker!—since few online services where around then. I would open up Microsoft FrontPage, write a blog post, save it, and then upload it to my website. This was the first iteration of my still-thriving blog, SmallBizTechnology.com.

Of course, years later most blogs are powered by WordPress or other hosting websites such as Medium.

Whereas the social networks are ideal for snackable bits of information, blogging is ideal for longer communication and is indexable by Google. Google is still by far the biggest network for searching. When people are searching for new shoes for their kids, tips on organizing a wedding, or advice for how to clean their home gutters, they're going to search on Google. If you, as a business person, post only on social media, you're missing out on the power of the Google search engine. It indexes blog content. So, yes, build your social following, but also publish a regular blog of great content. You can share this directly with your community through an email newsletter, and people searching on Google will find it as well.

Social media is transient; once you post something, it is buried under thousands of other posts filling your followers' news feeds within a few hours. You may tweet today about the bake sale, but a few hours later someone's looking at a silly cat video and your tweet or Facebook post has been pushed far down.

Blogging is powerful because Google is powerful and it more fully indexes what goes on websites. While it does in some ways index what gets posted on social media, it doesn't seem to index all of it, and it doesn't count what is posted on social media in its ranking of search results.

As a future celebrity CEO, you've got to use every tool in your arsenal, and SEO (search engine optimization) is one of those tools. Maybe you're the founder of a $4 million marketing agency and you're looking to expand your speaking and help orthodontists with their marketing. For sure, there are busy dentists who are looking to grow their practices and are looking for tips on marketing for dental offices. If you're creating a blog dedicated to all things MARKETING and DENTISTRY (see the two keywords), Google will index your blog and help dentists who are searching for marketing find your blog. Once they find your blog, they're apt to continue to click to reach out to you. See the power of SEO? Search is powerful, and the more great content you have online, the more people will find it through a search engine or because someone on a social network shared it.

With this understanding, it's important to blog on a traditional website, such as WordPress (the best option) or Medium, so that Google can index your content and your customers or potential customers can easily find it—with no other distractions or posts from others.

Let me further clarify: you *could* "blog" by posting regular content to LinkedIn or Facebook. However, in order to take full advantage of the power of Google to better rank your content in its search results, I highly recommend your actual blogging take place on a platform like WordPress or Medium. This is how a search engine sees your content.

While you *should* post snackable pieces of content on social media, you should also do a regular blog about this topic. Doing this means that people can find your expertise as they search Google and you can easily reference it and refer people to it. You could even have a domain name mapped to your blog—LocalFootballCoach.com or something like that.

Another reason why I like blogging is, if you can discipline yourself to blog and have an editorial calendar of content, you can use it as the start of your entire content-marketing strategy. With an editorial calendar you can write down different topics you might like to share with your community. If you're a landscaper, you might decide you'll do a blog post sharing tips on what people should do for their lawns every Monday. On Wednesdays, you'll share a blog post covering what they should prepare to do for the weekend. Maybe for Fridays you share a blog post on fun things they can do with the family to enjoy their lawns!

Here's a few tips to help you start or grow your blog:

1. Have a **theme** for your blog. The more niche it is, the better. I have SmallBizTechnology.com, which is all things technology for growing businesses and more. It's a bit broad, but it works. I also have SmartHustle.com, which is all about stories of entrepreneurs.

2. **Video** is powerful. Video you share on a social platform can often be embedded into your blog. Of course, you can also upload video to YouTube or Vimeo and embed it into your blog.

3. I also use **audio** quite a bit, especially on SmartHustle.com. I interview a guest and record the call, which is then downloaded to an MP3 file. I upload this file to an audio-hosting service, like SoundCloud. I get an embed code from SoundCloud and copy this code into the blog post related to the interview. Now I have a blog post summary of the interview and an audio interview as well. Talk about *engaging content!*

4. Build your **email list**. On your blog be sure to have a way for your blog readers to submit their email address to your email list or other opt-in email service. You can manually send them a regular email newsletter. You can also use a WordPress widget so that each time you create a blog post, those who have signed up get an email.

5. Use short and descriptive **headlines**. Maybe you are a health-and-nutrition consultant and you're writing a blog post about the benefits of eating nuts. Your blog post might be "6 Nuts to Eat Every Morning for a Healthy Heart." This headline is short but very descriptive. You want your headline to be as descriptive as possible for your audience. You also want it to be of relevance for Google to index and know what it's about.

6. Be **consistent**. If you're just starting out, don't expect to see results in just a few days. It can take several weeks, or even months, to see more traffic, more followers, or more email subscribers. But keep at it and be consistent.

7. You don't have to write your blog all by yourself. You can invite **guest bloggers** to contribute to your blog. Having a guest blogger gives you fresh content and takes all the pressure off of you. Plus, guest bloggers will want to share their featured blogs with their fans too! This cross promotion is a great technique to use.

8. Be **frequent**. You don't have to blog once a day, but I'd recommend that you blog at least once a week. If you're only blogging once a week, make sure it's thoughtful and highly informative to your audience.

Remember, your blog and your social content go hand in hand. Your blog content can direct to the content on your social networks. Your social content can direct traffic to the more in-depth resources on your blog. All of this can generate leads for your sales funnel and further marketing.

8

Podcasting

Creating a podcast is a great way to bring life to your personal brand. You could interview someone who is an expert in a particular field and influential in his or her market. It's a great way to shine the light on your own brand through collaboration with other professionals. Of course, your podcast can just be YOU, but most podcasts about any industry involve interviewing someone else.

Michael Stelzner, of Social Media Examiner, said, as a podcaster, the audience sees the expert you're interviewing imparting their wisdom to you; hence, your personal brand grows. Many people don't read, they might skim, and they don't read anything of substance. Video takes a higher quality of production to do it right, but people do like to *listen*, says Michael.

Over the past three years, I've interviewed dozens and dozens of entrepreneurs and other business experts for Smart Hustle Magazine, on SmartHustle.com. By interviewing the cofounder of video production company Animoto, my audience gets great content about all things video. But guess what? I get new listens and fans because Animoto will, most likely, want to share my interview with its followers. This is the power of podcasting, and interviewing other experts in general. You get great content and information to share with your community, and experts are going to want to share the interviews with their communities, further expanding your reach. And as Michael said, I look great, as my brand is now connected to Animoto. Make sense?

Don't be crass and only do interviews for this reason, or else it probably won't work well. Do the interviews because you *love* interviewing amazing people, while enjoying the benefits of collaboration.

To start your podcast, reach out to the experts you know who you feel will be open to letting you interview them. Once you get practice and gain traction, not only are you building your following but you will also be able to get more people to interview. Maybe your first interview will be a good friend who is an expert in his or her respective field. Maybe your two hundredth interview will be a well-known celebrity.

There are a variety of tools and resources you can use to record the audio for your podcast and share it.

Your audio need not be perfect, but it should be clear and enjoyable for the listener. I've done many of my interviews using just a smart phone, dialing into FreeConferenceCall. com, and recording the phone call. Then I download the MP3 file and upload it to SoundCloud. Other people use quality microphones—the sound quality does sound way better—and mixing software to equalize the voices and add in music!

There are hundreds of ways you can do your podcast. Do what works for you, have fun, and get better and better at it. Remember, the most successful interviews are when you're talking 20–30 percent of the time and the guest is talking the rest of the time. Be there to *facilitate* a conversation and have a dialogue. My style of interviewing is to have fun, make the guest sound smart, and have a short conversation. My friend Barry Moltz has that style of interviewing too. Of course, there are others who conduct lengthier interviews, but it's all about what works for *your* community.

9

Email Marketing: Build Your List

A few years ago, I received an email inviting me to speak at an event. The woman who invited me was not too familiar with me, but she was exploring her options. After she had hired me, she told me she had asked a colleague of hers, who happened to know me well, for his thoughts about me. He said, "I get Ramon's email newsletter all the time. Although I don't read every issue, hire him; he's good."

Email marketing is an easy way to stay at the top of everyone's minds within your community and to build a base of loyal fans. Social media has, deservingly, received a lot of the marketing attention in the last several years. You can "like" or "share" with a click or tap. You can use an emoji in a comment to express your reaction. But you can't do this with email.

Although people complain about all the email they receive, it's still the most efficient, most direct, and easiest way to communicate, especially about business. Email is, and will probably always be, a very important part of marketing one's personal brand.

With social media, you can get "likes," you can tag people, you can post and reply to comments, and you can have the visual experience of real-time communication. However, you don't *own* your audience on these platforms. Facebook, Snapchat, Twitter, etc., own the databases of users connected to you.

But with email, you own the database of *first name, last name, address, telephone,* and, most importantly, *email address.* You can reach out and email someone at any time and as often as you want. Of course, the people on your mailing list have the option to unsubscribe from what you're sending them.

I encourage every business professional seeking to build their personal brands to build their email lists—your database of customers and potential customers. Use an email newsletter to keep in touch with your fans, your customers, and your potential customers.

As you build this database, make sure you segment your customers. The more finely you segment your customers, the better you can target people. For example, if you only segment people by "state," you can only reach people by "state." If you segment people by "state" and "city," you can reach out and segment people even further. What if you add buying history, purchase preferences, and other demographic and psychographic information to the list as well? Here's how I use segmentation in my own business. There are people who live in Atlanta. So that's segmenting my community by geographic location, as some things I want only people in Atlanta to know about. I can also segment people based on their time in business. I can email just people who have been in business for less than a year versus a group of people who have been in business for five years or more. Or I might want to email just those people who are making $1 million or more in sales. The power of segmentation lets you communicate with your followers as precisely to their needs as possible. Instead of telling *everyone* about a sale you're having, you can just tell the 13 percent of people who are interested in that particular sale!

Using an email newsletter to periodically communicate with your fan base is essential to building and strengthening your personal brand. There's a number of great email marketing providers: Mailchimp, Aweber, Active Campaign, Emma, Constant Contact, Vertical Response, Infusionsoft, HubSpot, and many more.

I have been booked for speaking engagements and a zillion of other opportunities just from my email newsletter!

Your fans want to hear from you, and email is one tool that ensures you give them one more option in how to best hear from you. It's a way for you to break through all the clutter. While social media is a massive firehose of information overload, email still has an organizational flow to it, especially if you use good subject lines and you are emailing people who want to hear from you. Most business professionals wake up in the morning and still check their email.

I've learned over the years what it takes to build a great list and also use email effectively:

1. **You have information worth sharing!** At every appropriate opportunity, give people a chance to "click here and sign up" for your XYZ bit of information. If you're a sales consultant, let people

sign up for your "weekly sales tip newsletter."
You can refer to this in your social media
content, at events, on your business card, etc. Of
course, your website should have an email sign-
up form as well. DO NOT invite people to *sign
up for your email newsletter*; instead, invite people
to sign up for something useful to THEM. No
one wakes up in the morning to sign up for yet
another email newsletter, but a mom who is
nursing might sign up for a weekly list of tips for
how to better feed her child.

2. **Don't ask for a lot of information up front.**
    When people sign up for your email newsletter,
    make it easy for them. Ask for just the bare
    basics to get them signed up. First name, last
    name, email, and MAYBE zip code or one or
    two other bits of information to segment them
    in your database. You can use an email nurture
    system or marketing automation system to ask
    people to update their profiles in your database
    over time.

3. **Have a great subject line.** Maybe you're a local
    car-detailing company with a niche customer
    base of car enthusiasts; consider a subject line
    that reads, "How to get soda off your leather car
    seats—From Joe the Car Detail Guy." Don't use
    a boring subject line like "Car Detailing Tips."
    Each time you send your email newsletter, the

percentage of people who open it to read it is a direct result of how engaged they are by the subject line. People are BUSY—their attention is precious. Each email you send is a fight for that person's time and decision to open the email or not.

4. **Think about the MEAT of your email newsletter.** There are four zillion different ways you can publish your email newsletter. What's important is that you think of the reader and have content in it that is valuable and of interest to them. Your email newsletter could be very long if that's what your audience wants. In most cases, it is more efficient to have snackable pointers that people can quickly read, gain insight, and move on. You can use "click here for more" to drive people to a fuller article on your website.

5. **Frequency matters.** I suggest you send an email newsletter once every week or every other week. Less than that might be too infrequent.

6. **Mobile.** Don't just view your email newsletter on your desktop email program. Be sure to view it on your phone. The majority of your readers will most likely be viewing your email newsletter on their phones.

7. **Good design.** Your email newsletter need not be fancy, but it should be well designed. You can use a template from your email marketing provider. Also include some relevant and eye-catching photos!

One of the challenges I've faced in sending a regular email newsletter is knowing what to include in it. Here is what I've done to remedy that. Every two weeks, I look at my blog and my social media feeds and include in my email newsletter the best content from these resources. Remember, all of your fans are not seeing all of your content. If you're providing value to them, they'll love receiving an email from you.

People often tell me, "Ramon, we see you everywhere." Of course that's not true. But what they might not realize is that since I share valuable content so frequently and on a variety of platforms, I'm showing up in many places. This is important. Just sending an email newsletter is not enough. Just posting on Twitter is not enough. It's essential to give people a variety of options to hear from you. Also, someone might not see your tweet of just now, but will see the email newsletter sent next week. Frequency and multiplicity.

10

Apps and Hacks for Personal Brand Building

MacGyver succeeded because of his brains, but also because of the tools he had. This is the best time to be an entrepreneur who is intent on building a personal brand. Because of the Internet and the advancement of social media there is a myriad of tools, apps, and services. Many of these tools that help us save time, be more productive, and showcase our brands are built on top of the Internet.

Think about it.

To start your business, you can go online and be incorporated in minutes. You can build your website in about thirty minutes. Later that afternoon, you could be doing a live video broadcast. You can start collecting email addresses and reaching out to people directly.

There's a number of services you can use to have a virtual phone system for you and your team, and manage it all from your phone.

Your phone! Wow! You can run your entire business from your phone. Pay bills, send invoices, manage your team's tasks, see key performance indicators in a dashboard—the possibilities seem endless. There is an app and online software for everything you need to successfully start and grow your business.

This is a list of tools I have personally used and recommend to help you get started:

Image editing and image creation for social platforms and more: Canva is used to edit photos and images. PicLab is a great smartphone app to create more engaging images.

Video editing: Magisto, Animoto, Rippl (all mobile video editing apps); Adobe Premier Elements (a video editing software for your PC).

Task management: Asana

Event management: Eventbrite

Website building: Wix, Squarespace, WordPress

Blog building: Medium and WordPress

Email marketing: Constant Contact, Mailchimp, Emma

Marketing automation and CRM: Zoho CRM, Salesforce, ClickFunnels, ConvertKit, Infusionsoft, HubSpot

Social media management: Buffer and CoSchedule

Audio hosting for podcasts: SoundCloud

Collecting email addresses for your website: AddThis and SumoMe

Landing pages: LeadPages

Online forms: TypeForm and Google Forms

Conference calls and podcast recording: FreeConferenceCall.com

Testimonial management: Boast.io

Over the years I've found that with the combination of the right tools, my day became more productive, and I'm able to get more done in less time overall. The right tool can be the difference between spending thirty minutes on something or eight hours on something. It can be the difference between maximizing your digital presence or suffocating it. Also, don't be focused on "free." I hear so many business owners expressing their happiness that the tools they're using are free. Often when you pay for a product you get so much more out of it.

11

Digital Brand Building Stories, Tips, and Insight

RACHEL MICHAELOV, THE TAX EXPERT

Rachel Michaelov is the founder of Empire Tax Professionals. Over the past years I've seen her use Facebook to consistently share stories of how she's providing solutions to her clients. There are no sales (well, maybe a little bit), but she's using Facebook to share tips with us that she's giving to her clients to help them save money, get their finances in order, and so much more.

Doing this won't generate immediate sales for Rachel, but it *is* building her personal brand. It is planting seeds into the minds of the business professionals who will become fans of Rachel. In fact, I'm a fan of Rachel. I've mentioned her to you in this book! Rachel is building a fan base by posting regular content that's actionable, interesting, and useful. As I said before, all of these fans won't be customers, but over time, all she needs is for some of them to convert and become clients or to spread the word about her business.

Rachel's competitors, others providing accounting and bookkeeping services, might post something like this on Facebook: "Hi! Remember, stop by our office for a year-end accounting audit." Not bad. Or they might post "Before the year ends make sure you ask your accountant how you can maximize deductions for the year." However, when Rachel posts it's exciting and informative. She'll post something like "I just saved a customer $7,000 in taxes. Here's how we did it." Or she'll post something like this: "It's almost the end of the year. What are the things you're doing to minimize your taxes? Well, here's a few things I've been suggesting to my clients." See how something boring like taxes and finances can be made exciting and informative and catchy? You can do this for your business as well.

Adrian Miller, the Sales Trainer and Business Strategist

Adrian Miller is an expert in sales training and writing copy that creates sales. Because of her experience, she helps clients improve their social media engagement. Adrian is a good friend who, in addition to her consulting, founded a thriving networking group, Adrian's Network.[26]

Adrian shared these quick tips for social media success with me:

1. Stay visible with relevant content that spotlights you as a subject-matter expert and thought leader in your field.

[26.] http://www.adriansnetwork.com

2. Keep it "real" and relevant. Smart people can spot BS from a mile away.

3. Don't be afraid to include some personal story-telling. A post that I did about "What I Learned in Business from My Mom" garnered me more eyeballs and direct messages than many of my more "professional" posts.

4. Send out links to content you've written, and don't be shy about posting the links several times.

5. Experiment with posting a link or copying and pasting a (short) blog. Sometimes people dislike leaving the platform they are on to peruse what you have written. See what works the best for you.

6. Use pictures and videos as much as possible.

7. Ask people to share your content. Offer to share their content as well.

8. Social media is social. Don't sell lest you be thought of as "one of them."

9. Create and then reinforce your personal brand.

10. HAVE FUN.

You can see how anyone from any industry can leverage digital content to build a personal brand, to be engaging, to be informative, and to *educate* his or her fan base. Sure, it takes some effort to plan a strategy, but it's not rocket science. It's about having a mind-set to focus on how to best serve your existing customers, potential customers, and fan base! The tools you use are important, but more importantly, I hope you're understanding the process and the strategy of *how* to use the tools.

Personal Branding's Small Giants

I didn't want to leave this section without giving you a few more examples of how business owners, local consultants, and entrepreneurs are rocking their celebrity CEO status!

Diane DiResta is a presentation coach who helps speakers speak better. Since the summer of 2018, she's put out the third edition of her book *Knockout Presentations*. She also posts videos to LinkedIn. I've observed how Diane has gone from having a little digital presence to a LOT of digital presence. Gary Vaynerchuk posts lots of content every day. Most of us can't do this, as we don't have a team to help us get that done. However, people like Diane, with limited time and resources, can do one useful video a week.

Know what your audience wants, and be very specific in the information you provide to them. Diane's information is all about being a better speaker; your information is going to be about what's important to your audience. Success in using digital media is all about *frequency*—

posting to Twitter several times a day and to LinkedIn at least once every few days. Of course, it's got to be *quality*. This sounds simple, but she's building her brand and becoming the go-to source for speakers and communicators by continually updating her social platforms. I vividly remember one of her videos about how to smile for photographs. Instead of saying "cheese!" which creates a fake smile, Diane suggested saying "money!" giving you a more natural smile.

Jimmy Newson is another amazing professional. His specialty is inbound marketing, generating leads for a product or service. Jimmy speaks on a regular basis at the New York Public Library; each audience attracts around thirty to fifty attendees. Is Jimmy going to be *globally* famous doing this? No, but by consistently giving insight (for free) to an audience of business owners, Jimmy continues to enforce his celebrity CEO status. Not only is his name blasted to thousands of inboxes in library emails, he's also reaching a very defined and niche audience of experts who need his insight and his services.

Let's look at Joe Apfelbaum, the most connected guy in New York City! Joe's known for taking selfies—lots of selfies. I have selfies with Joe from various events over the years. He's also known for connecting with people through LinkedIn and promoting others overall. Many people think personal branding is all about self-promotion, but Joe's style maybe works even better. He promotes other people, and over time they're going to be promoting him, in one way or another. Hey, I'm promoting him now!

My friend Daniel Johnson has an upstart company, Get Up Inc. Daniel motivates people to better health and a better life. He's using Instagram in a powerful way to show people, un-edited and in near "real time," how they're working out and how he's motivating them. Furthermore, Daniel has live events where he brings people together. There's something about live events that will always be endearing. We can do AR, VR, and every other *R*, but the best *R* is in REAL life.

Elaine Pofeldt recently launched a book, *The Million-Dollar, One-Person Business*, chronicling the journey of people who are one-person businesses but making over $1 million a year. Elaine's not a social media butterfly; however, she's used the power of live events quite successfully to generate interest in her book and build her own personal brand.

While social media is an easy and important way to build your brand, there are many other things you can do to build a fan base, to build your brand, and get *recognized!*

Jen Slaw is a speaker, entertainer, juggler, and mom to an adorable toddler—who's learning how to juggle. While you might think that anyone with these talents and skill set has it easy, Jen has to work hard to build her personal brand, just like everyone else. What she's done is not just to juggle and speak but to do "huggles." When Jen performs, she gives a gentle hug to someone and juggles while hugging.

Building your personal brand is about telegraphing what can make you special, what can make you different, to the audience. It's about how you stand out.

PART III

FROM SMALL SCREEN TO STAGE

12

The Art of Public Speaking and Communication

One big part of building a personal brand is public speaking. Communication and public speaking include being able to communicate one-on-one, speak to thousands on stage, or speak to a few dozen professionals at a local chamber of commerce event.

In a few hundred words, I can't teach you how to communicate or speak like Tony Robbins. However, I encourage you to take the time to develop your public-speaking skills. There are countless free resources available online. Take it one step farther with the numerous courses, classes, seminars, and conferences out there that can put those skills to practice. I recommend Toastmasters, which is a wonderful organization to help you perfect the art and science of public speaking.

From my over twenty years of public speaking, here are a few tips to get you started:

1. **Perfecting clear communication takes time.** I've been a professional speaker for over twenty years, and I get better each time I'm on stage.

2. **There are different types of speaking.** Someone who is exceptional at communicating one-on-one will have a different skill set than someone who excels at speaking to an audience of thousands on stage.

3. **Know what you're talking about.** Don't try to speak about leadership if you know nothing about leadership and have no experience in it.

4. **Elevate your voice.** Many people think they speak loud and clear, but they don't. You can get voice lessons in how to elevate your voice and speak with power and clarity.

5. **Own the stage.** Don't stand in one place like a potted plant, but don't walk aimlessly around the stage like a puppy! This takes practice. I've seen amazing speakers who pace around the stage. This is annoying to the audience, and you might get dizzy!

6. **Be a storyteller.** Be sure to use examples and a story to convey your thoughts and build empathy and trust with the audience.

7. **Connect with the audience.** If the audience is your "friend," if they smile with you and laugh with you, then you're well on your way to a great speech.

8. **Prepare.** Don't just walk onto a stage and talk. Know your audience. Know the room. Practice your presentation.

9. **Communication is first and foremost about listening.** If you're on stage speaking for sixty minutes, you need to "listen" to the audience ahead of time and get to know as much as you can about your audience. If you're speaking one-on-one or in a small group, take the time to ask questions and listen to the needs of the people around you.

10. **Have good diction.** I know I speak way too fast, so when I speak, I think conscientiously about *s-l-o-w-i-n-g* down. If your accent is unfamiliar to the audience you're speaking to, be aware of this.

11. **Energy and passion.** People can *feel* your excitement. If you're boring, they'll be bored. If you're excited, they'll be excited. You can telegraph your emotion in your body language, facial expressions, and tone of voice.

12. **Think about your words.** There are many executives who communicate via Twitter or phone calls or from stage and wish they could take back their words. Words matter. Words have meaning. Think before you speak.

13. **Pause.** Pause for effect. Think about your favorite comedian—mine is Steve Harvey. Do you notice how he pauses for emphasis or to get your attention?

Think about someone whose words you heard and who captivated your attention, who caused you to want to hear more and to take action. Sometimes it was in the context of a major need or event—such as Martin Luther King Jr. and the civil rights movement. However, for most of us, it's not about something so grand. It's about getting someone to buy an annual consulting contract, convincing a mom to try out your daycare service, or getting a group of teens to do better in their internships. We communicate all kinds of ideas to all kinds of people in all kinds of scenarios.

The more you boost your personal brand, the better you can convey ideas, excite your audience, and get them to take action.

Diane DiResta,[27] mentioned earlier as a personal branding small giant, is a communication expert and shared with me her advice on the importance of communication:

Speaking is the new competitive advantage. You can no longer be without this skill. Speaking is a leadership skill.

[27.] http://www.diresta.com

And how you speak is your personal brand. You can actually manage or change perception by the way you present yourself. People who have good presentation skills have more success in job interviews, get more promotions, make more money, and are more influential.

I coached a CEO of a Fortune 1000 company. He wanted to convince the executive committee to fund the building of a vaccine facility. The cost would be $300 million. There was no guarantee of success, and then there would be three years of clinical trials. He got the approval, and that $3 million investment turned into a $1 billion success. Without powerful presentation skills he would have lost the opportunity and the company would have lost a great opportunity.

13

Event Production

What makes a celebrity CEO a celebrity CEO?

Remember what we shared very early in this book? You want to build a base of fans. You are a celebrity, and you want to be perceived as one. You want your fans to have opportunities to connect with you, and nothing builds a stronger connection than being present, *live and in person*!

By hosting or holding an event, you are taking a big step toward solidifying your celebrity brand. My first big event was in 2006 at the Small Business Summit. I organized it with my then partner Marian Banker, and I've been doing it every year since!

The Small Business Summit brings together hundreds of business owners and great sponsors every year. So in 2006 I was just your average business owner. I was speaking, blogging, and doing some other things here and there. My brand was okay.

However, the day I held the Small Business Summit, gathering together hundreds of attendees, it put me on a platform, a *branding platform*, above my peers. I started my journey of being the Celebrity CEO. Today, years later, the conference, now entitled the Smart Hustle Small Business Conference, is still going strong!

Why?

I had a stage—a real, physical stage—but also a "stage" for my brand. An event to showcase that social media alone can't match. Think about the Super Bowl or other marquee events. These events are smorgasbords of sensory delights and experiences. You need to have your own marquee event. Events can provide an experience to your community that only an in-person event can do. They can SEE you live and in person. They can HEAR you (and others). They can TASTE the food during networking. They can FEEL someone else through a handshake or hug. An event solidifies you as a celebrity CEO!

The media has attended my conference, as well as VIPs in my industry and big brands. In-person events give you a platform that social media alone just can't match. Events take time to organize. They take money to put together (getting the space and food are the biggest costs). But if they are done well, they are a *huge* boost to your brand.

Let's pretend you're a local sales coach and you make your living giving sales training to companies. I would assume that there are many other sales coaches in your area, and for sure in your country, doing just about exactly what you do. If you were to organize the "Miami Sales Conference and Workshop," I bet there aren't many of your competitors doing big events.

By hosting an event like this, you bring together your clients and potential clients; some local media might come to cover the event, and you invite a few local celebrities in the field of sales training. Now *you* have a stage. You are the celebrity. You'll put your face and bio on all the handouts; you'll be one of the featured presenters. A good event gives you credibility, visibility, and legitimacy.

See what I mean? *Do ya feel it?*

Events take you from "average" to "celebrity." I warn you again—it is *hard* work. It is an expense. But events are an important pillar to separate your brand from everyone else.

Another opportunity for events is through partnerships. I've had sponsors (who help pay for the event) from leading brands. I've been blessed to have speakers who have appeared on Shark Tank attend my events. The rich opportunity for collaboration and partnerships is a huge part of producing an event as well.

You can do a big event with thousands of people, or you can do a small event with twenty to fifty people.

Here are a few tips on event production:

1. **Marketing:** I like to leave at least a month and a half to market an event. The bigger the event the more time you need to market it in advance. For my annual Smart Hustle Small Business Conference, I market it throughout the year! The best way to market an event is to use your own lists. This is the cheapest way. Use your email list and your social media followings to share your event with others. Remember, most event registration occurs at the last minute. It can be

very scary to wonder if anyone will show up, and you'll never know—until they do. Partner with other individuals and organizations who can help you market your event to their networks.

2. **Event registration:** Use a tool such as Eventbrite, Meetup or Zoho's Backstage, to manage your attendee list and ticket sales.

3. **Event venue:** I've used many different spaces for my events. From conference rooms in private companies to conferences spaces for rent, and more. You can even work with local restaurants or bars to use their space during the day or when they're closed. Breather.com is a nice service for finding space to rent by the hour. If you've never been to the venue before, go there at least once to be sure the venue is what you want. Hotels are a nice space, but pricey. Maybe you want a hip space with brick walls, but does this space have the equipment you need to produce a great event? Do you have to hire staff and bring in additional equipment?

4. **Fee or free tickets:** There is no right or wrong way when it comes to a free versus a fee event. A free event gets those who are not as serious, for sure. You might get a hundred people to sign up, and assume half of them won't show. If you charge for the event, you can expect most of the people who

register to attend—no one wants to lose money. Charging for the event (even just five dollars) increases the percentage of people who will show up. One more thing: by setting a ticket price you add **value** to the event. You tell the market that your event is worth something.

5. **Agenda:** Who speaks at the event is another important consideration. The more well known your speakers are, the more interest people will have in attending your event. I try to have a "draw" at my event, that one person I can get whom everyone in my industry might want to see. At my annual Smart Hustle Small Business Conference I've had Seth Godin speak on several occasions. Remember, most people want to speak at an event to get on *your* stage and boost their *own* brand. Oftentimes, you might not have to pay for a speaker.

6. **Know your speakers:** You want speakers who add *value* to your event and respect you and your audience. There have been a few times I was *mortified* by a speaker who boringly read his or her presentation or by a speaker who was just selling something to the audience. Get speakers who want to share and contribute to the success of your event.

7. **Event title:** The name of your event and the title of your agenda items are important. Maybe you're having an event on how to sell your business. Instead of an event entitled "How to Sell Your Business," what about "How to Scale and Sell Your Business"? See how a couple of words in the title add a bit more spice to the event name?

8. **Staffing:** If you're doing a *very* small event, you can do the event yourself. The bigger the event, the more important it is to have staff who can help you manage the event. It is important, especially for a bigger event, to have professional event staff. You don't want your cousin or your poor momma to staff the event. You want people who are professional, can manage a crowd, and know the art of event staffing.

9. **Budget:** It's important to manage the money you're spending for an event and the money you hope to bring in. Using a simple spreadsheet, you can put down your budget items so you can do your best to anticipate costs and income. You can expect money from sponsors and from attendee ticket sales.

10. **Energy and excitement:** It's important to ensure your event has LIFE! The audience wants to feel energized, not bored. Think about whether or not you should hire or partner with someone who can be the event host or emcee.

11. **Giveaways:** One of the fun parts of my events are the giveaways. I work with sponsors to give away computers, books, pens, and everything in between!

BIG TIP: For the last few years, I've started promoting my attendees in the premarketing of the Smart Hustle Small Business Conference. When attendees register, via Eventbrite, I have their registration sent to Infusionsoft. From Infusionsoft, I email each attendee and ask them to tell me about themselves. With this information I promote THEM via social media. They love it and others love it. Guess what? FOMO (fear of missing out) creeps in, and others sign up too!

Here's a few other things to keep in mind: Who are you serving? Who is your audience? Are they looking for in-depth and detailed insight? Do they want lots of networking? Do they want to meet sponsors? Your number one metric of success will be your attendees. Serve their needs and your event will go well. Build your agenda around the needs of your audience, NOT your own needs. During the registration process you can survey attendees to get a sense of what topics they want to hear about and whatever else is of importance to them.

Of course, before even considering the event ready to open up, it's essential to know what your audience wants at an event. It's important to know what they'll get out of it and what's important to them. After your first event, *ask* for critique. While you want praise, you want to hear the *toughest* critique from attendees so you can be sure that the next event is even better!

How Can You Speak at Events

I'd be negligent if I did not offer some advice for how YOU can speak at events. While it's great to produce events, it's even better in some cases to speak at events. I started speaking for free at SCORE—http://www.score.org—the nonprofit organization, funded in part by the United States government, that provides free counseling to small businesses. From this beginning and by leveraging the power of personal branding that I'm sharing with you in this book, I have built a successful, paid speaking business and work with well-known brands and agencies across the country.

First, start speaking for free at small events. Your local chamber of commerce is a great place to start. Be involved in your local association, and ask to speak on panels. As you do this a few times, people will see what a great speaker you are (right?) and you'll be invited (or you can ask) to speak more and more.

For most of you, speaking for free will often help you gain new clients and get added visibility for your business. If you're interested in being a paid speaker, I highly suggest you start attending your local National Speakers Association events—http://www.nsaspeaker.org. Tell them Ramon from the NYC chapter sent you.

The MOST important thing about getting more and more speaking engagements is just be the BEST at what you do. There are all kinds of tricks and tips I and others can give you. But if you're not what I call a "stage-crushing speaker," you're speaking opportunities will be limited. The best of us—Jay Baer, Seth Godin, John Lawson, and

Mike Michalowicz—are exceptionally great speakers, and we are in demand. If you're among the best, your speaking career will soar.

14

*Video Brings Your
Brand to Life*

The marketing manager of a billion-dollar Fortune 500 company said to me, "Ramon, I've watched all your videos. I know you love burnt pancakes and bacon . . . We'd like to hire you to host a new show."

I was shocked (just a bit).

This executive saw my quirky (and serious) videos and knew that she wanted to leverage the dynamism she observed in my videos for her company.

If I had not have been consistently producing videos, this encounter might have never happened. You can leverage video in a very powerful way to personalize your brand and humanize your expertise. Business cards don't buy from each other; humans buy from humans. Showcasing yourself in a video is a great way to attract attention and "sell" yourself.

There are two main types of video you should have:

1. **A profile video** that encapsulates your professional expertise and shows you in the best light. It's a

video that shows your accomplishments, such as any books you've written or anything of value you've created. It should show you speaking and include any other elements that express how amazing you are. This video might only be updated once every two or three years. Some people call this a sizzle video. This video should be professionally produced and give people who are interested in you a quick taste of who you are, how you work, and how you are able to help them.

2. **Educational videos** are a must have. These are videos you produce on a regular basis to educate your audience and keep you in the forefront of their minds. You can record and share these videos from your smartphone. You can see the many videos I produce by checking out my profiles on Facebook, LinkedIn, or Twitter. Educational videos can be fun or serious, but they are intended to provide *information* or *something of value* to the viewers to help them in some way. You create them with some regularity. Some of the titles of my videos include "Can You be Happy in the Rain," "Why Luck Is Overrated," "Follow Up without Being a Jerk," and more. Think about your audience and your industry. What questions are they asking? What answers do they want? Your educational videos should be about these things.

So how can you produce your videos? It's very easy to shoot great video. Here are a few tips from my play book:

1. You can use **your phone** or you can **buy a professional DSLR camera,** which will have better image quality and other features. I've been using my phone much more than my professional camera, as the phone quality of video is fit for online viewing. If it were being broadcast to TV, I'd need a higher-quality image, most likely. The modern phone in your pocket (one that's no more than two or three years old) produces video that's good enough for most purposes.

2. Have **good lighting.** Be sure that the light is *behind* the camera facing you so you're well lit. You don't want to be in shadow. You should be clearly lit and visible.

3. **Audio** is important. You want people to hear you clearly. Be sure to shoot your video in a quiet room or have an external microphone to capture the best sound. There is a variety of solutions you can use to capture great audio. I have a shotgun microphone. It is a long microphone that looks like a small umbrella or a baton one might use in race. This microphone is great for isolating and focusing on the sound right in front of it. You have to hold it toward the person's mouth or have it clipped to your video camera. I also use a lavalier microphone,

which I can clip onto someone for an interview in a quieter location.

4. Now it's time to **edit** your video. You can hire someone or you can edit it yourself. There are many great video editors you can find on freelance websites, such as Upwork.com (great for all sorts of freelance professionals). I also use an app, Magisto, which is great for editing videos on your phone. Adobe Premier Elements is a simple and cheap-enough video editor that you can use on your desktop computer! It's best for fuller video editing with various tracks and other features.

5. Many people watch video with the sound turned off, so you might want to **add captions** to your videos so that people can read what you're saying without having to have the audio on. You can use a service, such as Rev.com, that will take your video and provide a caption file for a dollar per minute of video. You then take the caption file and upload it to Facebook or YouTube (or other services) with your video file. After your video is processed, when people play it, they'll see captions in your video and can "hear" what you are saying without the sound.

6. Include a **call to action**. End the video by asking people to follow you on social media, watch

another video, visit your website, or take advantage of a special offer.

After you shoot and edit your video, be sure to share it far and wide—place it on social media, your website and blog. Remember, the more great videos you produce, the more your personal brand is strengthened and developed. The more videos you do, the more credible and more comfortable people will feel about you.

STOP!

I know some of you reading this are already thinking about how you have to get things "just right," how perfect your video needs to be, etc. I've been doing video for many years, and although my goal is always to do my best, every video is not always going to be perfect. If your message is clear and you can be seen and heard clearly, you'll be just fine. In fact, sometimes being too perfect is a turn off. Clients, your community, like to see "real" and authentic. This is why reality TV is such a hit. Of course, reality TV is scripted, but it's the closest we'll get to seeing the "real life" of the Kardashians or famous people in Atlanta, etc. As you consider using video to build your personal brand, just be consistent. When I first launched #AskRamonRay, a live show I do on Facebook on Sunday evenings, it was not perfect. In fact, it's *still* not perfect, but I'm out there, engaging with my fan base, and the viewership is growing. That's what matters!

My friend Roberto Blake has a lot of great content all about video production.

Posting your video on YouTube is powerful. YouTube video marketing is an industry all on its own, and it's a skill set. Use a descriptive, keyword-rich headline for your YouTube videos. Be sure to fill out the description. Remember, YouTube is owned by Google, so its keywords and descriptions are so important and will help to get your video in search results.

Video is the NUMBER ONE reason why my brand is growing and why I am a celebrity CEO. If you're creating good video, your fan base will increase, people will share your videos, and people will want to work with you. You'll find that, like me, you'll be *chased down* more and more by people interested in your business, your products, and collaborating with you. That's the power of video!

I guess this is why Hulu, Netflix, YouTube, and TV are so popular. This is why all the social platforms are investing so much into video. Humans love seeing other humans in action, and video is the only way to do that if you're not there in real life.

15

Write and Publish a Book

When my third book, *Facebook Guide to Small Business Marketing*, was published, my personal brand went up several notches. I was invited to speak at more places, had more media interviews, and even my smile got bigger and better!

A book, similar to an event, is a tool that gives you credibility, visibility, and legitimacy. It's a hook you can use to get media attention and share with others. A book is a great tool to use to seal a business deal, win a new client, or say "thank you" to an existing client.

There are two parts to writing and publishing a book. One part is actually writing the book. This takes time and thought. In fact, as I type these words, I'm thirty-one thousand feet in the air on a six-hour flight back to the East Coast. However, it's the easiest part of the book production process. You can write the book yourself or get help writing it.

The second part of the book-writing process is the **marketing** of the book. It makes no sense to write a book if those whom you wish to read the book are not aware of its existence. Long before you write your book on paper, make a plan to market it. You should be building an email list, attracting interest on social media, and using every resource you can to generate publicity for your book.

A book is also a great hook to use to get media attention (TV appearances, quotes in newspapers, etc.) and to be invited to speak at events and more. A book is a tool that screams loudly that *you are credible*. It's a tool that adds to your legitimacy.

Most speakers don't write books to make a lot of money, especially with their first books. Write the book to build credibility in the market and among your peers.

Here are a few more things to consider:

1. If you don't have a fan base, a large email list, or a large social following, don't write a book. First, build your fan base and your community, and then write a book that you can market to this community.

2. If you've never written and marketed a book, do an e-book first. Do something that's substantive—maybe it's thirty or fifty pages—then market it so you can get traction with your community. After a successful e-book launch, where you can learn a bit, then focus on your first book.

3. My first book was self-published. It was a great experience to discipline me about **writing** and **marketing**. To become an author, you no longer

have to have your book published by a "real," or formal, publisher. In the age of self-brands, like being the Celebrity CEO, self-publishing your book can work just fine.

4. Why a publisher? A publisher is great because they provide editors, a book designer, and get your book distributed through all the major channels— Amazon and book stores! But they won't do *all* the work to market your book. It's in your hands to market to your community and a new audience.

5. Book design matters. Think about how your book will look on a bookshelf or how it will look in a lineup of ten books, scrolling up or down on an Amazon app. Your cover should be designed to quickly attract attention.

I will also say that Seth Godin's advice for authors is well worth the read.[28]

[28.] http://bit.ly/sethadvicetoauthors

16

Get Media Coverage:
Your 15 Minutes of Fame

I remember being in the green room at Rockefeller Center before going to a taped episode of *Your Business* with JJ Ramberg of MSNBC. I was nervous, but I was ready. Since then, I've done what seems like hundreds of interviews on podcasts, radio, TV, and other outlets.

You can get your fifteen minutes of fame, as well, if you plan for it and make it happen. Here's an example of planning for media coverage and making it happen:

It happened to me in December 2018. *The New York Times* came out with an article about how a black doctor was helping a passenger on an airplane, but the staff didn't believe she was a doctor, and it took some convincing and showing of credentials. The article explained that, many times, white doctors have helped passengers in distress on an airplane and didn't have to go through a lot of explaining or provide proof of their credentials. I contacted the writer and shared my story of how I've been given car keys to park cars and coats to hang. People assume I'm "the help," I presume because I'm black. Several days later, my head shot was featured in *The New York Times*. Let's rewind. I saw a story where I thought I could fit in. So you have to keep your eyes open for opportunities. Second, I was able to contact the reporter and sent a pitch that caught her interest.

Most of us love watching the news, or we have our favorite cable show. These news segments all have one thing in common. They have an expert who is commenting on a particular news item or topic of discussion, or they have someone who *is* the news story or focus of the information.

Let's say there is a news story about the government's new tax laws. The reporter will feature either an expert on how the new tax laws affect small business or a business owner who is speaking about how the new tax laws affect his or her business.

This is the opportunity for YOU. You are an expert, right? You're an expert in *something*. Are you able to comment on how a particular news story affects you or your business?

Understand where you fit into this media equation—are you the **expert** or the **story**? For some story angles, you might be the featured expert who is commenting on a headline. For other angles, you might be the focus of a news story, or a part of it.

Here are my four big tips to gain media attention (without being the subject of a scandal) and to have a journalist interview you:

- **Have a story.** To get the media to take interest in you and your business, you must have something to say. Going back to our tax law example, maybe your story will be the three things every business owner needs to do to lower their taxes.

Maybe your story is how the new tax laws enabled you to hire more employees (or caused you to have to fire employees). Just asking a journalist to interview you for her next newspaper article is not enough. You've got to clearly explain *why* her audience will be interested in what you have to say.

- **Target the media.** Once you have your story, get to know the media. Know whom to pitch to and why journalists want to cover your story and share it with their readers. Remember, every radio station or news outlet might not be a fit for your story. Be selective and picky. Don't just look at the "top tier" media. Just because your local Fox News affiliate is covering the launch of Apple's latest product doesn't mean they want to cover your business. Maybe the local association publication would be a better fit for starters.

- **Pitch your story.** Next step is to share your story with relevant journalists. Get them interested in how your story can benefit their readers or viewers. When you pitch them, be an asset, be helpful. You are *not begging* them to talk to you; you are offering them an opportunity to speak with you and have some useful content for their audience.

- **Be persistent.** Many times when you don't hear from a journalist (or blogger or podcaster), they are not ignoring you, they are just busy. I know my inbox is filled every hour with dozens of emails to go through. And these are *not* emails from my team or friends. These are unsolicited emails from public-relations professionals pitching me on this or that story for me to cover their clients.

Media attention is not just about getting on the front page of *The Wall Street Journal* or having an hour-long talk on *60 Minutes*. There are hundreds, if not thousands, of blogs and podcasts that would love to share your story, your knowledge, and your expertise. Indeed, it's a great adrenaline rush to brag to your friends that you were on CNN or Fox Business (as I've been). They won't know about the little blog about entrepreneurship or accounting or lawn care. But if that little blog is where your audience is, it might be even better than being featured on Oprah or Dr. Oz.

Timing is another important aspect of getting media attention. For example, what are the big stories that the media, in general, wants to cover between November and December? Thanksgiving and Christmas! Right? So your pitches to the media should focus on thankfulness, gift giving, etc.

What are the big events, occurrences, and important dates in your industry or that are important to your customers? What are the international events that are happening that you might be able to leverage? In my industry there's SXSW, held every March in Austin, Texas. There's Salesforce Dreamforce with 170,000 plus attendees every fall in San Francisco. There's Small Business Saturday, held in November. There's Small Business Week, held in the spring and produced by the Small Business Administration.

Having a **story** to tell is essential, and you might be struggling with what kind of story to share. Maybe you think you have no story. But here is a list of a few items to consider that make great stories:

- **Statistics and trends:** What if you could start a pitch with "Did you know that 87 percent of Americans sleepwalk?" If you are a sleep doctor, that might just get you an interview!

- **Commentary on the news of the day:** Mainstream news organizations' first priority is to cover the major news of the day—politics, crime, finance. It's tough to get a foothold in this vicious cycle, but it's possible with persistence and by building relationships with the news producers.

- **Charity work:** Nothing warms a TV studio's heart more than some puppies running around. Maybe you've volunteered to help a local veterinarian get their finances in order and can bring some cute puppies to the studio as part of the story. Maybe you help a local nursing home redesign its recreation room. Charity work is a great hook to get the media to pay attention.

- **Your customers:** Remember, you might not have an interesting angle for a story, but your customers may. If they can weave you into their stories, it's a win for you and a win for them. Oftentimes, as an influencer, I'll work with a brand to represent it in a news story. Online software may be boring, but by featuring me, a successful entrepreneur and high-energy, fast-talking, raised-in-New-York-City person, the online software comes to life with excitement.

A strong personal brand is strengthened even more when you have the media featuring you in some way. This is why media attention is important and can boost your celebrity CEO status.

Having a book published, speaking at events, or having been covered by the media before—these are all items that make you more credible and desirable to the media.

So how do you start actually pitching to the media? Here are a few ways I've done it:

1. **Email.** Journalists are flooded with emails. The big way to ensure *your* email has the best chance of being noticed (and opened) is to have a great SUBJECT LINE. As a reporter (or blogger, etc.) is scanning through hundreds of emails, it's the subject line of the email that is most important. Of course, your pitch inside the email must be good too.

2. **Twitter.** Most journalists use Twitter as a way to glean information and scan what to cover. Pitching journalists via Twitter is very effective. Over

time, you might build a "Twitter relationship" with a journalist!

3. **In-person meeting.** I've met many journalists in person. Nothing makes a great connection like a firm handshake and a warm smile. If you can get a journalist to know, like, and trust you, you're well on our way to a chance at getting media coverage.

These are few ways you can start to build relationships with journalists. As you build the relationships, remember to provide VALUE to them. Keep their audiences in mind. Once you secure an interview, **prepare.** Learn the art of speaking in "sound bites," know how long the interview will be, and know the audience. Do your homework. You have ONE chance to get this right. Leaving a good impression can lead to an invitation to return again and again.

17

Get Help.
Hire Expertise.

When I was working full time at the United Nations, one of my fledgling side hustles was growing. This was good because my business was indeed growing, but it was bad because I still had a full-time job, which was getting in the way of my entrepreneurial aspirations. I had to hire help. A few weeks before, I had met an administrative assistant, who, after I hired her, helped me grow my company for many years.

Help is essential.

I've always relied on a great team to help me grow my business—be it organizing events, managing content, or other things. You'll want to hire for two main reasons: **Hire for expertise.** Your expertise, what you do best, is limited. You can probably do one or two things very well. For the things you don't do so well, you can learn to do them a bit better, but in the long term your business will benefit from hiring someone who can help you.

For example, I often hear this advice to business owners: you can use *this* or *that* tool to do graphics work on your own. Some image and video editing you can probably do on your own. But consistently I've found that the work of a professional designer is nearly impossible to match. A professional designer has the expertise from pouring in the five or ten or more years of experience that you'll never be able to match—unless you want to become a designer. You have years of experience in what you do, right?

The second reason you'll want to hire is to save you time. Over the years, I've spent what seems like hundreds of hours poring over WordPress code or HTML in attempts to tweak or update various areas of my website. Sometimes I end up getting things updated or fixed, and sometimes I don't. However, every time I work with my website developer, Andigo Media, they get it solved quickly and perfectly, much better than I can. I waste time, a precious commodity, when I fiddle with things that I should leave to experts who can solve it much faster than I can.

Sure, you have to pay for their expertise. But your time is so, so, so valuable. Here are a few things I've learned over the years in hiring the right person. It works most of the time.

1. **Know what you want.** Be sure you really know what your needs are, what your challenges are. It's hard to hire someone if you're not clear how he or she can help you.

2. **Have a clear job description.** Even though someone might just be "working on your website,"

it helps to have a short job description. This way, what you expect of them is clearly documented. If you need to hire someone else, you can do so.

3. **Measure for success.** Be sure to benchmark, to measure, the success of the person you've hired. Have regular meetings, in person or on a phone call or via email. Ask yourself (and them), are they fulfilling their responsibilities to you and the job? Are you fulfilling your responsibilities to them?

4. When using an online talent site, such as UpWork, **use a clear job description.** Having "Web designer needed" is too broad. How about "Lover of HTML and WordPress Needed for Nonprofit"? This kind of job description is not only eye catching, but I find it attracts a better type of person—sometimes.

Should you hire an **employee** or a **contractor?** An employee is great when you have steady work and really want someone who is fully dedicated to you. For most of the work I do, I'm quite fine using contractors. They work when and where they want, and through clear communication (email) and a task management tool, we get a lot done and my business grows.

You want an experienced contractor who has only you and a handful of other clients. Not too many, or they're too busy to work with you, and not so few that they have to skimp around for jobs just to make ends meet.

Conclusion

Over the past few years, I've consistently generated hundreds of thousands of dollars per year—all because of a strong personal brand. It's not easy, it's hard. Very hard. It takes discipline, a dose of self-promotion, and a desire to educate your audience and build a fan base.

If you follow the principles in *Celebrity CEO* and use the tools I've given you (or discover your own better tools), you'll find that you will be well on your way to having clients chasing after you and being able to raise your prices and choose how you want to live.

You don't want a strong personal brand just to stroke your ego or just to be on TV. No, you want a strong personal brand to *grow your business*, as demonstrated by an increase in revenue, profits, and more time to spend as you see fit.

All the tools in the world won't do you any good if you're not **frequent** and **consistent** in how you share your content.

Building a strong personal brand is not a sprint, it's a marathon. It takes times time and dedication. Rarely does someone have an overnight personal brand. If you consider Dave Ramsey, Gary Vaynerchuk, and Steve Harvey, they are all professional who, over time, have built strong brands due to the content they've produced.

Indeed, you might not get millions of followers on Twitter or be featured on the front cover of a popular magazine. However, you can be well known to the professional community that matters most to you and indeed be a celebrity CEO!

Want to be in contact with me? Email me at

ramon@smarthustle.com. I'd love to hear from you!

CPSIA information can be obtained
at www.ICGtesting.com
Printed in the USA
FSHW020001170919
62084FS